HOLD FAST TO JESUS
AN IN-DEPTH STUDY OF HEBREWS

ELIZABETH BAGWELL FICKEN

Hold Fast to Jesus © Copyright 2019 by Elizabeth Bagwell Ficken
Printed in the United States of America
W & E Publishing, Cary, NC

Scripture quotations identified as NKJV are from the Holy Bible,
New King James Version, copyright © 1979, 1980, 1982, Thomas Nelson, Inc.
Publishers. Used by permission. All rights reserved.

Scripture quotations identified NASB are from the
New American Standard Bible © The Lockman Foundation, 1960, 1962, 1963, 1968,
1971, 1972, 1973, 1975, 1977. Used by permission.

Scripture quotations identified NIV are from the *New International Version*,
copyright © 1973, 1978, 1984 by International Bible Society.

Scripture quotations identified NLT are from the Holy Bible,
New Living Translation, copyright © 1996. Used by permission of
Tyndale House Publisher, Inc., Wheaton, Illinois 60189. All rights reserved.

Scripture quotations identified The Message are from *THE MESSAGE*.
Copyright © by Eugene H. Peterson, 1993, 1994, 1995.
Used by permission of NavPress Publishing Group.

Scripture quotations identified ESV are from The Holy Bible, *English Standard Version*® (ESV®), copyright ©2001 by Crossway Bibles, a publishing ministry of
Good News Publishers. Used by permission. All rights reserved.

Scripture quotations identified HCSB are from the *Holman Christian Standard Bible*®, Copyright 1999, 2000, 2002, 2003, 2009 by Holman Bible Publishers. Used
by permission. Holman Christian Stand Bible®, Holman CSB®, and HCSB® are
federally registered trademarks of Holman Bible Publishers.

Scripture quotations identified as NET are from *The NET Bible*® Copyright © 2005
by Biblical Studies Press, L.L.C. www.bible.org. All rights reserved.

"Do you know Jesus?" Gospel presentation from Sonlife Classic.
Copyright © 2009 Used by permission.

Cover: Jeannine Klingbeil
Tabernacle illustration: Bethany Shinn

*This study is dedicated to my parents, George and Susan Bagwell,
who are a testimony of holding fast to Jesus.*

*I am deeply thankful for the team of supporters who have prayed, advised, provided retreats,
and spurred me on through the writing process: Kathy Peterson, Emily Nelsen, Sandi Terrill,
Ellie Ficken, Christen Merithew, Dr. Randall McKinion, Pastor Scott Wylie, my husband Wade,
and the women in my Bible study classes.*

*Now may the God of peace who by the blood of the eternal covenant brought back from the dead the
great Shepherd of the sheep, our Lord Jesus Christ, equip you with every good thing to do His will,
working in us what is pleasing before Him through Jesus Christ, to Whom be glory forever. Amen.*
Hebrews 13:20-21 [NET]

ISBN-10: 0-9905933-6-3
ISBN-13: 978-0-9905933-6-2

TABLE OF CONTENTS

Introduction		5
My Bible Story		6
Do You Know Jesus?		7
Helpful Hints		8

Lessons:

1.	The Introduction	Hebrews 1:1-4	10
2.	Jesus Christ—the Son of God	Hebrews 1:2-4	15
3.	The Exalted Jesus Christ	Hebrews 1:5-14	19
4.	The Dominion of Jesus our Lord and Savior	Hebrews 1:7-14	24
5.	The First Warning	Hebrews 2:1-4	28
6.	The Pastor's Message	Overview	33
7.	Jesus Christ—the Son of Man	Hebrews 2:5-9	38
8.	Jesus Christ—Made like Us	Hebrews 2:10-18	42
9.	The Greatest Of All Time	Hebrews 3:1-6	46
10.	Beware of Unbelief: The Second Warning	Hebrews 3:7-19	51
11.	A Sabbath Celebration	Hebrews 4:1-13	57
12.	God Has Spoken	Hebrews 4:12-13	62
13.	An Intriguing Introduction	Hebrews 4:14-16	66
14.	What We All Need	Hebrews 5:1-11	70
15.	On to Maturity	Hebrews 5:12-6:12	75
16.	A Very Sober Warning	Hebrews 6:4-6	80
17.	A Lot to Think About	Hebrews 6:4-12	85
18.	Trust the Promises of God	Hebrews 6:13-20	91
19.	Mysterious Melchizedek	Hebrews 7:1-24	95
20.	Our Personal Perfect High Priest	Hebrews 7:25-29	99
21.	The Sanctuary, Sacrifices, and Covenants	Hebrews 8:1-13	103
22.	The Importance of the Old Way	Hebrews 9:1-10	108
23.	Once for All Time	Hebrews 9:11-14	113
24.	The Promised Inheritance	Hebrews 9:15-22	118
25.	Do You Want to Go to Heaven?	Hebrews 9:23-28	121
26.	The Sacrifice of Christ	Hebrews 10:1-14	126
27.	A Total Transformation	Hebrews 10:9-17	131
28.	Unrestricted Access	Hebrews 10:19-25	135
29.	Hold Fast to Hope	Hebrews 10:23	139
30.	Team Spirit	Hebrews 10:24-25	145
31.	A Very Sober Warning—Repeated	Hebrews 10:26-31	149
32.	Now Faith	Hebrews 11:1-3	155
33.	Entering the Hall of Faith	Hebrews 11:1-40	159
34.	Father Abraham and the Faithful Patriarchs	Hebrews 11:8-22	165

35. Moses and More Faithful Followers of God	Hebrews 11:23-31	170
36. Unlikely Heroes of the Faith	Hebrews 11:32	174
37. Unnamed Heroes of the Faith	Hebrews 11:32-40	179
38. Endure the Agony	Hebrews 12:1-3	185
39. For Our Good	Hebrews 12:4-11	189
40. Clear Instructions	Hebrews 12:14-17	193
41. Unshakeable	Hebrews 12:18-29	198
42. Precious Doctrine and Practical Conduct	Hebrews 13:1-4	202
43. Until Then	Hebrews 13:15-25	206
44. Jesus is Better	Reflections on Hebrews	213

Endnotes	218
Prayer Requests and Praises	222
Other Studies by Elizabeth Bagwell Ficken	234

INTRODUCTION

Dear Friends,

Each writing of a Bible study brings me great delight as I see God lead me through the process. Each one is written with whole-hearted, desperate dependence on the Lord. I must have His power and presence and direction. I write by faith through the exciting discoveries and through my insecurities, hesitations, and difficult circumstances.

The book of Hebrews is about trusting Jesus—alone—when life is good and when it is hard, challenging, and painful. It is an eloquently written book with beautiful explanations of the sacrifice of Christ and the radical results of our salvation: forgiveness, sanctification, and free access to the throne of God! It also contains many intriguing topics which may be unfamiliar to the 21st-century reader.

I have been amazed at the life circumstances that God has allowed me to experience throughout my writing of this study. He provided retreats away from home for intensive study and writing. And when no place away was available, He gave me the focus and discipline to write at home in the midst of regular schedules. Hebrews begins with praise to God for sending Jesus His Son to earth and shortly after beginning this study, I enjoyed welcoming new life—our first grandchild—into our family.

The book of Hebrews teaches us to trust in the finished work of Christ until we reach heaven, to live on earth by faith, with hope and love. Throughout the letter, there is a call to endurance through the hardships of life until we reach the heavenly city. The Lord is allowing our family to embrace this perspective all the more as we walk the journey that comes with the diagnosis of ALS for my mother. The day she shared her diagnosis with me, she said: "Are you jealous that I will see Jesus before you do?!" Of course I am! I'd love for Jesus to come in the clouds and gather us from life on earth all at the same time.

My mother is living out the message of Hebrews, trusting in Jesus' sacrifice as the all-sufficient solution to our great need. He is the source of eternal salvation. He has entered through the veil into the holy presence of God on our behalf. He is our Great High Priest always interceding for us. And He opened the way for us into the very throne room of God where He lovingly, abundantly gives us grace to help in times of need.

Some of the Hebrews who received this letter were struggling with their faith in God because of the hard circumstances of their lives. The truths spoken by the Holy Spirit in this letter give us everything we need to understand that we can depend on Jesus. He is the steadfast anchor fixed in Heaven who gives us hope and strength.

I am so thankful for the incredible calling of God to study the Bible deeply, slowly, and in intimacy with Him. He has given me the precious opportunity to stand under waterfalls of truth and explanation and enlightenment. I hope through this workbook to share some of that life-giving water with you.

Waterfalls become rivers which then flow to the oceans. There are several sea-faring terms in Hebrews which emphasize our critical need to pay close attention to our heading so that we don't drift off course. Study Hebrews with me and be reminded to hold fast to Jesus.

MY BIBLE STORY

I love my Bible! But I have more than 10 of them on my bookshelf, so which one do I love and use to read and study? I'd like to answer that question with my Bible story.

The earliest Bible that I remember reading was a children's New Testament Living Bible. It was a birthday present from a friend when I was eight years old! I tried to read the book of Revelation but didn't get very far. The next special Bible that I received was a black (faux) leather King James Version with Susan Elizabeth Bagwell engraved in gold letters on the front. This was from my parents and it was my church Bible. I don't remember reading it at all, but I must have taken it to Sunday School with me because I found a Psalm 23 bookmark in it. That was to become the first well-known Scripture to me.

When I was fourteen (ninth grade) I began using a paperback Bible which my father felt was an excellent translation. The New English Bible is not very well known, but, it was the Bible that made me begin to know God's word. My Sunday school teacher actually made us read and study Ephesians; I underlined verses and took it with me to Bible studies in high school.

My first Bible with cross-references and helpful notes was the Ryrie Study Bible in the King James Version. A friend took me to the Baptist Bookstore and I experienced picking out a Bible for myself. It was bound in dark blue (faux) leather and Elizabeth Bagwell was engraved in silver lettering. I bought it after high school graduation and used it for my quiet times and Bible study and sermon notes for about 10 years—through college and early marriage and the births of my children! It was falling apart and the bookbinder recommended a durable covering: blue canvas. I call it my blue jean Bible now!

Then I became aware of the New King James Version and decided it would be nice to leave behind Thee's and Thou's of the Old King James... so I bought The Woman's Study Bible NJKV. It was refreshing to read God's truths in a new translation in a Bible that had clean pages for me to make new notes on. Familiar verses were lovely and overlooked verses began to stand out as they had not done before. The changing of Bible translations became a new adventure for me.

I own and have read through the Bible in the NIV, NLT, NET, NAS, NKJ, ESV, and HCSB translations. It is important to me to have a Bible with helpful study notes; historical, cultural information; word study definitions; and appropriate cross-references. The layout of the Scriptures on the pages is important too! It just has to feel right! I have used the Archeological Study Bible and the Life Application Bible, but have enjoyed the Nelson Study Bible and the Holman Christian Standard Study Bible more.

I've received precious Bibles as gifts as an adult, including a friend's German Bible, my grandmother's 100 year old Bible that my mother remembers from her childhood, and one that I call my "coloring Bible" which allows me to meditate on, color, and delight in Scriptures which have been illustrated.

Jesus loves me this I know, for my Bible tells me so! I love God's Word and I love my Bible — whichever one I may be reading at any given time.

DO YOU KNOW JESUS?

This is the most important question in this study. Please notice that I didn't ask you if you know about Jesus. But do you know Him, personally?

The Bible teaches that God loves you: "For God so loved the world . . . that He gave His one and only son that whoever believes in Him will not perish, but have eternal life." John 3:16 ^{ESV}

And it teaches that God wants you to know Him personally: "Now this is eternal life, that men may know Him, the only true God, and Jesus Christ whom He has sent." John 17:3 ^{ESV}

But . . . people are separated from God by their sin: "Your sinful acts have alienated you from your God" Isaiah 59:2 ^{NET}

Sin causes us to miss the very best for our life: "Jesus said, 'I came that you might have life and have it to the full.'" John 10:10 ^{NIV}

Sin causes us to face death and judgment: "The wages of sin is death." Romans 3:32 ^{NAS} "Those who do not know God . . . will pay the penalty of eternal destruction away from the presence of the Lord." 2 Thessalonians 1:8-9 ^{NAS}

But there is a solution! Jesus Christ died and conquered death for you! We deserve death and judgment, but Jesus took upon Himself the punishment for our sins, so that we could have a personal relationship with God: "For there is only one God and one Mediator who can reconcile God and humanity-- the man Christ Jesus. He gave his life to purchase freedom for everyone." 1 Timothy 2:5-6 ^{NLT}

It's not enough just to know this. Each of us by faith must receive Jesus Christ if we want to know God personally: "To all who have received Him—those who believe in His name—He has given the right to become God's children." John 1:12 ^{NET} "For it is by grace you have been saved, through faith—and this not from yourselves, it is the gift of God." Ephesians 2:8 ^{NIV}

The ABC's of faith involve:
<u>Acknowledging your need</u>—admitting you have sinned and desiring to turn from sin. (1 John 1:8-9)
<u>Believing Jesus Christ died in your place</u> and rose again to be your Savior—providing forgiveness for your sins. (1 Corinthians 15:3-4:17)
<u>Choosing to invite Christ</u> to direct your life. (Romans 10:9)

Your desire to have a personal relationship with God can be expressed through a simple prayer like this: "Dear Lord, I want to know You personally. Thank you for sending Jesus who died in my place and rose again to be my Savior. Please forgive my sins. I am willing, with your help, to turn from my sins. Come into my life and lead me. Amen."

For illustrations and more information, go to **KnowHimPersonally.com**

HELPFUL HINTS

If you are new to in-depth Bible study. You will need a Bible. Please feel free to use the version of your choice. There are many translations. If you are using a Catholic Bible or a Jewish Old Testament it will be helpful for you to also use a modern version of the Bible which includes the Old and New Testament.

I recommend the following versions which are available for free at online Bible study websites, in smartphone and tablet apps (see recommendations on the next page), or for purchase in Christian bookstores. They are usually referred to by the letters in parentheses.

New King James Version (NKJV)   New American Standard Version (NASB)
New International Version (NIV)   Holman Christian Standard Bible (HCSB)
English Standard Version (ESV)

This study was written using multiple translations. I have found that I can gain an understanding of the meaning of verses by reading other versions of the same passage. Two other popular Bibles are *The Message* and the New Living Translation (NLT); these are both wonderful versions for comparative reading but are not as appropriate for in-depth study.

Planning time for your lesson. Set aside a specific amount of time to work on the lesson. One lesson may take 30-45 minutes depending on your familiarity with the Scriptures. You may want to do the lessons in shorter increments of time, depending on your schedule and personal preferences. I find that I absorb, retain, and apply the message of the Scriptures better when I am not rushed.

Please begin your study time with prayer. Ask the Holy Spirit to give you understanding of God's Word, as it is promised that He will do according to 1 Corinthians 2:12-13: "Now we have received, not the spirit of the world, but the Spirit who is from God, that we might know the things freely given to us by God, which things we also speak, not in words taught by human wisdom, but in those taught by the Spirit, combining spiritual thoughts with spiritual words." I have given you a reminder at the beginning of each lesson.

Observation, interpretation, and application. The Scripture readings, activities, cross-references and word definitions are all placed in the order which is most appropriate to your study. It is best to follow this order if you can, rather than skipping steps or setting steps aside to be completed at a different time. The order follows the inductive study process: observation (what the Scripture says), interpretation (what the author intended, what the Scripture means) and application (what difference the Scripture makes in your life). You will be doing the research, cross-referencing and summarization of the truths of each passage. When you finish a study of a passage, you will have gleaned more understanding on your own than you will find in some commentaries!

Looking up Greek word definitions. One of the activities included to help you understand the correct interpretation of the scripture is discovering and considering the definition of a word in its original language. Please make sure that you look up the definition of the word in its original language, not the definition of the English word. You will be given a prompt like this:

>**Faith: Strong's #4102**
>**Greek word:**
>**Greek definition:**

There are several ways you can look up the words given.

- You can google the Strong's reference number (Strong's 4102) and your web browser will give you links to the definition.
- You can go to an online Bible study website (recommendations below) and use their free reference materials. Look for "study" tabs, "lexicons" (this is what Hebrew and Greek word dictionaries are called), "concordances" and "original language" tools. There are search boxes where you can type in the Strong's reference number. Use G before the number for Greek words (G4102).

    >studylight.org   blueletterbible.com   searchgodsword.org

- You can download free Bible study apps for your smartphone and/or tablet. I use **MySword** which allows me to go to a passage and click on the Strong's reference number next to the word. Try a few different ones and see what you like best.
- You may have some great resources on your own bookshelves! Enjoy using books like *Strong's Exhaustive Concordance* and *The Complete Word Study Dictionary* by Spiros Zhodiates.

If you have trouble, it would be better to skip the exercise rather than filling in the English definition.

It's about your head and your heart. My hope is that you will read portions of Scripture and gain an understanding of what is being communicated through them so that you can consider how to apply the truth of God's Word to your life. I have tried to make the study "user-friendly" and I promise that I don't ask trick questions. I do want to make you think hard sometimes though! I hope you won't get overwhelmed. Do what you can, a little bit at a time. The reward of knowing our holy God through His recorded word far outweighs the time and effort of study.

Prayer requests and praises. You will find pages at the end of this workbook which provide a place for you to write out a personal prayer request. If you are studying with a group, it would be helpful to reflect on your personal prayer request before sharing it with the group. Keep your requests brief and personal. This page is also a place to record the prayer requests of others.

LESSON 1: THE INTRODUCTION
HEBREWS 1:1-4

Hebrews. The book of Hebrews. The letter to the Hebrews. The name itself is surprising. In the New Testament, books are named according to their authors (Matthew, James, Jude) or the churches or people to whom the letters were sent (Romans, Ephesians, Titus) or based on the content of the book (The Acts of the Apostles and The Revelation of John).

Weren't the Hebrews the people of the Old Testament?

Was this a letter written to them? And who wrote it? Why does it refer to Melchizedek, sacrifices, and the blood of bulls and goats?

These are usually the first questions considered when discussing the book of Hebrews.

> Hebrews is a delight for those who enjoy puzzles. Its form is unusual. Its setting in life is uncertain, and its argument is unfamiliar.[1]

I hope I haven't scared you away from the study of this brilliant, intense, and critically important book of the Bible! I am so excited to study this book because even though a few historical questions remain unanswered, the most important eternal truths are explained.

How did the author describe his recipients and his writing, and what was his desire according to Hebrews 13:22?

We'll learn a little more about the author and the recipients as we get further into our study. Even though there is uncertainty about who they were, this book is certainly important for us today. We've got concerns, challenges, and troubles, just as the recipients of this letter had. Circumstances and cultural pressures often tempt us to look for tangible escapes to something we think is "better than" faith and hope in Jesus.

Please hear the message of this letter! Jesus is better . . . . He is better than anything that you might look to for help. And that's why we must: Hold Fast to Jesus!

As we study, we will do as the unnamed author urged us in Hebrews 12:2. We will fix our eyes on Jesus. We will see Jesus Christ, the Son of God, in all of His majesty and glory, in His suffering and sacrifice, and in His compassion and care for us.

And if we heed the warnings given by the author, we will hold firmly to the faith (Hebrews 4:14), we will hold unswervingly to the hope we profess (Hebrews 10:23), we will run with perseverance the race that lies before us (Hebrews 12:1).

When we have completed our study, I hope that you will see the beautiful portrait of our Savior and the great salvation He has provided for us. If the book of Hebrews is a puzzle, then only a few inconsequential edge pieces will be missing!

Let's get started. The author was certain that the Holy Spirit speaks the words of God.

Please make it your regular practice to pray for understanding and enlightenment from the Spirit, and the response of obedience to the Lord.

^{NET} **Hebrews 3:7** Therefore, as the Holy Spirit says, "Oh, that today you would listen as He speaks!"

Please read Hebrews 1:1-4. This is the introduction to the whole book.

We will take an in-depth look at these profound truths, but first, let's respond in worship to our God and our Savior. Write your praise for who God is and what He has done based on verses 1-4.

As I reflect on these verses, I am overwhelmed with amazement and adoration for my God and my Savior. When we look at these statements more closely, we will see that they communicate incomprehensible love and grace.

These verses set the stage for the explanations and exhortations of the whole book, which most consider to be a written sermon. The author has caught our attention with a magnificent thesis statement. With eloquence in the original Greek and beautiful words in any translation, the theme of the sermon is laid out.

Let's list the statements which are the doctrines of our faith:

Hebrews 1:1: Long ago, God spoke _____

Hebrews 1:2: In these last days, God has spoken _____

Hebrews 1:2: God appointed His Son as _____

Hebrews 1:2: Through His Son, God made _____

Hebrews 1:3: The Son is the _____ and the

_____

Hebrews 1:3: The Son sustains _____

Hebrews 1:3 The Son made _____ and then He

_____

Hebrews 1:4: The Son is superior to the _____

Hebrews 1:4: The Son has inherited _____

Based on these observations, what would you say that you know and believe about the following:

God

Jesus

God's relationship with man

Sin

The introduction to this sermon tells us that there is a God; He speaks to us; He knows our need; He has met our need through His Son. There is a glorious, transcendent God in Heaven who communicated to mankind in many ways and then communicated to mankind through Jesus. God intends for us to know Him intimately! Through our study of Hebrews, we will see that Jesus has made the way for us to enter into the presence of God.

Now, and in the next lesson, we will look at Hebrews 1:1-4 more closely and try to grasp the profound truths presented in these verses.

^{ESV} **Hebrews 1:1** Long ago, at many times and in many ways, God spoke to our fathers by the prophets.

What were some of the times and ways that God spoke to "the fathers"? Briefly note who God spoke to, how He spoke if it is mentioned, and what He said, based on the references below.

	Who God Spoke To	**How God Spoke**	**What God Said**
Genesis 2:16-17			
Genesis 6:13-14			
Exodus 19:17-19			
Numbers 12:6-8 (2 ways God speaks)			
Job 28:28			
Daniel 9:20-22			
Zechariah 1:1-4			

God gave clear instructions and promises, didn't He? One of the critical points that the author of Hebrews will point out is that the fathers were disobedient, even rebellious, against God's word. They serve as an example of what not to do. One commentator describes the first 4 chapters of Hebrews as "a very short history of the disobedient people of God." [2]

Let us make note of the fact that God spoke in the past. And there were people who heard Him who ignored, rejected, or didn't believe His word.

The writer of Hebrews will give several warnings throughout his message. What is his greatest concern, according to Hebrews 12:25?

As special as it is to receive the word of God, it is sobering as well. When God speaks, He means what He says! He is our holy God who is to be reverenced and obeyed. His word is given to us so that we might know Him intimately and relate to Him correctly.

We also need to realize that the words which God spoke to the fathers pointed to Jesus. While we refer to the "Old Testament" and the "New Testament," they must be seen as one book, proclaiming the same gospel of salvation by grace through faith in Christ. The newest Bible on my bookshelf is entitled "The Complete Jewish Bible" and that is how we should view every Bible. The writer of Hebrews shows throughout his many quotes of scripture that Jesus is the fulfillment of and completer of all of God's promises.

What is your response to the words of God in the Old Testament?

What is your response to the words of God through Jesus, recorded in the gospels?

What is your response to the words of God given in the letters of the New Testament?

I hope you are already intrigued by the book of Hebrews and eager to learn more from this written sermon. It's a message from the heart of a pastor and the heart of the Lord.

LESSON 2: Jesus Christ—the Son of God
Hebrews 1:2-4

What is your favorite praise song or hymn about Jesus? The first verses in Hebrews may contain phrases from an early Christian hymn. This passage, which serves as an introduction to the sermon, focuses our attention on the exceptional, matchless distinction of Jesus Christ. There is no one greater than He. Please prepare to humbly and thankfully consider His greatness.

Please pray that you will hear and heed the word of God and the direction of the Holy Spirit.

Please read Hebrews 1:1-4.

Compare the statements in verses 1 and 2 by filling in the blanks below.

Previous revelation (Heb.1:1)	**Final revelation (Heb. 1:2)**
Timing: in the past	**Timing:** _____
Speaker: God spoke	**Speaker:** _____
Recipients: the fathers	**Recipients:** _____
Agents: through the prophets	**Agents:** _____

> These clauses articulate the basis for any sound biblical theology by affirming the continuity between God's OT revelation with its focus on Sinai and His final revelation in Christ. At the same time, they anticipate what will soon be elaborated: Christ is God's final word that fulfills and thus surpasses His previous revelation.[1]

This is doctrinal and theological but it is also doxological! That means it's what we believe about God and it should prompt us to give glory to God! God the Father has communicated everything that we need through His Son. Jesus Christ is the One that all the Old Testament saints were waiting for; He has come, and He has fulfilled all of God's promises.

What does 2 Corinthians 1:19-20 say?

God has spoken to us "in a Son" as the original Greek says it. Jesus as God's Son, as the one intimately related to God, is emphasized here. Jesus the Son of God is greater than the prophets of old who were mere men.

Let's acknowledge and admire the greatness of Jesus Christ. There are seven descriptions of His person, His work, and His status given in the introduction to Hebrews. They give us more theology, specifically Christology (the study of Jesus Christ). If we don't know who Jesus Christ truly is, then we will not know God as He truly is, and our faith will be flawed and our behavior will be defective.

Note the phrases that describe Jesus next to the categories below and note the corresponding truths in the cross-references given:

1. **He is Son** (Hebrews 1:2) –

    Psalm 2:7-8

2. **He is Pre-existent** (Hebrews 1:2) –

    John 1:3

3. **He is Deity** (Hebrews 1:3) –

    John 1:14

4. **He is the Revealer of God** (Hebrews 1:3) –

    Colossian 1:15

5. **He is Sustainer** (Hebrews 1:3) –

    Colossians 1:16-17

6. **He is the High Priest** (Hebrews 1:3) –

    Leviticus 16:30

7. **He is Exalted above all** (Hebrews 1:3) –

    Ephesians 1:20

Hebrews 1:3 contains a few rare and distinct words which have influenced some scholars to see it as a phrase from a hymn. Let's continue to think about the greatness of Jesus as we look at their meanings.

Please look up the following words. Helpful hints for researching Greek words are given on page 8-9:

Radiance: Strong's #541
Greek word:
Greek definition:

> This word denotes the radiance shining forth from the source of light. Just as the radiance of the sun reaches this earth, so in Christ the glorious light of God shines into the hearts of men and women.[2]

Representation: Strong's #5481
Greek word:
Greek definition:

> In Jesus Christ, there had been provided a perfect, visible expression of the reality of God.[3]

Purification: Strong's #2512
Greek word:
Greek definition:

> By making purification for sins the Son of God has accomplished something incapable of achievement by anyone else.[4]

Majesty: Strong's #3172
Greek word:
Greek definition:

> He is the Prophet through whom God has spoken His final word; He is the Priest who has accomplished a perfect work of cleansing for His people's sins; He is the King who sits enthroned in the place of chief honor alongside the Majesty on high.[5]

While we are still contemplating these profound descriptions of our exalted Savior Jesus Christ, let's make sure that we have the right perspective about the relationship of God the Father and God the Son. We are considering our Triune God.

Jesus, as Son, and as the reflection of God the Father, is not inferior to God, but is one with Him. However, being the exact representation of God does not mean that Jesus is not distinct from God. He is distinct, a separate person of God who is Three in One.

That's probably still confusing. The Trinity—our God who is Father, Son, and Holy Spirit, God in three persons—is mysterious. The book of Hebrews will show the distinct actions of the Godhead throughout its chapters.

It's time to get personal. Because Jesus came to speak to **us.** Look at the 7 doctrinal descriptions of Jesus on page 16. What you believe determines how you behave. Reflect and make notes of how you are responding, or how you should respond, to these truths about Jesus.

Because He is the Son of God –

Because He is the Pre-existent One –

Because He is Deity –

Because He is the Revealer of God –

Because He is Sustainer of all things –

Because He is my High Priest –

Because He is Exalted on High –

> The opening statement in Hebrews introduces us to the heart of the book as a whole: God has something to say to the church, and that message focuses preeminently in the person and work of the exalted Son.[6]

The author of Hebrews sums up his introduction in Hebrews 1:4 and gives us a transition to his upcoming comments. Beginning here and continuing throughout his writing, there will be an emphasis on how much better Jesus is than anything or anyone.

Please write your praise to Jesus based on Hebrews 1:4 as a closing for today's lesson.

LESSON 3: THE EXALTED JESUS CHRIST
HEBREWS 1:5-14

We've had a profound beginning to our study, which set the stage for the whole message of Hebrews. The author was keenly aware of our need to see Jesus as He truly is, in all of His pre-eminence and excellence. The next passage reinforces the description of our exalted Christ with Old Testament scriptures.

Please pray to hear and heed the word of the Lord as the Holy Spirit gives you understanding of it.

Please read Hebrews 1:5-14 below. I've given you the passage with the quotes of Old Testament verses indented so that they will be obvious to you.

ᴱˢⱽ Hebrews 1:5-14

⁵For to which of the angels did God ever say,

> "You are my Son, today I have begotten you"?

Or again,

> "I will be to Him a father, and He shall be to me a son"?

⁶And again, when He brings the firstborn into the world, He says,

> "Let all God's angels worship Him."

⁷Of the angels He says,

> "He makes His angels winds, and His ministers a flame of fire."

⁸But of the Son He says,

> "Your throne, O God, is forever and ever, the scepter of uprightness is the scepter of Your kingdom. ⁹You have loved righteousness and hated wickedness; therefore God, Your God, has anointed You with the oil of gladness beyond Your companions."

¹⁰And,

> "You, Lord, laid the foundation of the earth in the beginning, and the heavens are the work of Your hands; ¹¹they will perish, but You remain; they will all wear out like a garment, ¹²like a robe You will roll them up, like a garment they will be changed. But You are the same, and Your years will have no end."

¹³And to which of the angels has He ever said,

> "Sit at my right hand until I make Your enemies a footstool for Your feet?"

¹⁴Are they not all ministering spirits sent out to serve for the sake of those who are to inherit salvation?

Before we consider the purpose of these scriptures, I'd like to point out that this passage tells us a few things about the writer of Hebrews. He is extremely knowledgeable about the Old Testament and aware of how to interpret the Scriptures when they apply to Jesus Christ the Messiah. The verses that the writer uses are messianic, which means that they pointed to Jesus and would find their complete fulfillment in Him.

Another characteristic of the writer of Hebrews is his unique style of quoting Scripture. He refers to almost every Old Testament reference as being spoken by God or the Holy Spirit, rather than attributing it to Moses, David, or the prophets. Think back about his opening statement that God spoke in times past. He demonstrates that truth throughout his writing by telling us what God has said and what God continues to say through the God-breathed texts he quotes.

Now let's consider the purpose of the Old Testament quotes in Hebrews 1:5-14. Commentator George Guthrie states that "teachers of Scripture built support for a theological position by stringing together various Old Testament texts. The desired effect was to offer so much evidence that your listeners shook their heads in agreement with you by the end of these quotations." [1]

Please number the Old Testament quotes on the previous page (#1 - #7). And I've highlighted each one in a different color in my notes, but that's up to you! Next to the appropriate verse above, write the reference given below:

#1 – Psalm 2:7

#2 – 2 Samuel 7:14

#3 – Psalm 97:7

#4 – Psalm 104:4

#5 – Psalm 45:6-7

#6 – Psalm 102:25-27

#7 – Psalm 110:1

Briefly note above, next to the Old Testament references, the main idea of the verse given. (Who is it about? What is the point? What name is given to Jesus based on the verse?)

Please look back at the previous lesson, page 16, and notice that there were 7 descriptions given about the greatness of Jesus. These descriptions are supported in the 7 Old Testament references that refer to the Messiah (except Psalm 97:7 and Psalm 104:4).

Write the characteristic or title of Jesus next to the appropriate verses above.

Hebrews 1:5-14 supports the writer's introductory description of Jesus and gives us even more truth about Him. Let's not miss a thing.

What is Jesus called in Hebrews 1:6?

How is Jesus described in the following verses?

Romans 8:29

Colossians 1:15

Colossians 1:18

The term firstborn carries several nuances. In the Jewish culture, the firstborn son received a greater inheritance and more privileges than his brothers. The term is also used to describe rank, priority, and honor.

> He is called "the firstborn" because He exists before all creation and because all creation is His heritage. The title may be traced back to Psalm 89:27, where God says of David (and in general of the Davidic king): "I will make Him the firstborn, the highest of the kings of the earth." [2]

Look back at Hebrews 1:5-14 quoted in your workbook on page 20. Draw a bracket around quotes #1, #2, and #3. This is the first grouping of scriptures given to make a point. Based on Hebrews 1:5-6, how does the writer show that Jesus is superior to angels?

Even though this passage is highlighting the supremacy of the Son of God, it also gives us a little information about angels. They are fascinating creatures and are part of God's good creation.

What does God do with His angels, based on Hebrews 1:6 and 1:14?

> Angels are created, heavenly beings, who primarily function as messengers for God, revealing His will or announcing key events (Gen. 19:1-22; Ex. 3:2-6; Judg. 2:1-5; Matt. 1:20-24). They also serve to protect God's people (Ex. 14:19-20; 1 Kings 19:1-8; Acts 12:7-11).[3]

Why does the writer draw so much attention to the superiority of Jesus over the angels? Were the readers worshipping them instead of Jesus? Possibly, but there is no clear evidence to support that idea. Consider the following explanation instead:

> In Hebrews 2:1-4, the author casts the angels in a positive, though inferior, role. This positive role is basic to the rhetorical argument that the hearers need to take seriously the revelation delivered through the Son. "Why the angels?" has nothing to do with the worship of them and everything to do with the execution of a skillful argument on the part of our author. [4]

> To be sure, the listeners had a high regard for and interest in angels… At this time Jews placed great emphasis on angels as intermediaries between God and people. They were seen as exalted beings who functioned as heavenly emissaries. This fact makes the rhetorical argument all the *more powerful.* The audience's respect for the role of angels provided a reference point from which to speak of the much higher position and, therefore, authority of the Son of God. [5]

What are angels doing in the following verses?

Matthew 4:10-12

Luke 1:26-27

Luke 15:10

Luke 22:39-43

Acts 12:7-8

Revelation 5:11-12

What do you think about angels? Are there any adjustments that you need to make in your perspective about them?

As I mentioned earlier, angels are fascinating. But they really don't even compare to our superior Savior. Let us fix our eyes on Jesus by once again reading the description given of Him in Hebrews 1:1-7. We will look at the rest of the details given about His distinction in the next lesson.

What is the most meaningful statement to you about Jesus in Hebrews 1:1-7?

LESSON 4: THE DOMINION OF JESUS OUR LORD
HEBREWS 1:7-14

Are you beginning to grasp the importance of knowing the fullness of who Jesus is? The writer of Hebrews is intentional and thorough in his description of the Son of God. In Chapter 2, we will see the personal application that he makes based on the greatness and supremacy of our Savior.

But first, there are still awesome and wonderful essentials about Jesus to acknowledge from the Old Testament messianic passages quoted in Hebrews 1.

Please pray that you will hear and heed the word of God and depend on the enlightenment of the Holy Spirit.

Look back at Hebrews 1:5-14 quoted in your workbook on page 20. Draw a bracket around quotes #4, #5, and #6. This is the second grouping of scriptures given to make several points.

According to Hebrews 1:7, the angels are created beings and servants. According to Hebrews 1:8-12, how is Jesus different and superior to the angels?

Did you notice that Jesus rules and angels respond? And Jesus creates but angels are creatures? Another critical doctrine that can be seen in this grouping of verses is that Jesus never changes—He is immutable. Unchanging. His throne is forever and He has always been in existence. The heavens and earth will be changed, even angels change form to do the will of God, but Jesus is the same.

How does the writer say it in Hebrews 13:8?

From the beginning to the end of this book, the truth that Jesus Christ is unchanging is emphasized. Life's circumstances change but Jesus does not.

Let's get a preview of how the writer will encourage us based on the truth of Jesus' unchanging nature. Summarize the impact of Jesus' immutability given in Hebrews 7:23-25.

What a comfort it is to trust that Jesus is who He is—always! All that He is, He always is. For our mortal lives on earth, the only thing that we can be certain of is change. But Jesus is on His throne in Heaven as our Savior, God, Lord, and High Priest always and forever.

Are you experiencing any changes in your life? They might be exciting or they might be excruciating. How can considering the unchanging nature of Jesus help you accept, adjust to, and endure changes in life?

In our description of Jesus, we have not yet noted that He is the anointed King. How does Hebrews 1:8-9 describe His reign?

Let's get another preview of what is to come. In Hebrews 5:6, we will learn that Jesus is "a priest forever according to the order of Melchizedek."

Read Hebrews 7:1-3 and note what the name Melchizedek means.

I have to admit that I really like the name Melchizedek! For years I was baffled by the meaning of Hebrew names, but then a class on the Hebrew language helped me decipher them!

We will learn more about Melchizedek later.

What we can learn from these verses now is that Jesus is a king of righteousness, just as Hebrews 1:8-10 declares. He will always do what is right.

Look back at Hebrews 1:5-14 quoted in your workbook on page 20. Draw a bracket around quote #7 and the last verse. This is the third grouping of scriptures which highlights that Jesus is superior to the angels.

Hebrews 1:13 is a partial quote from Psalm 110 and brings the writer's point to a climactic conclusion. What is the ultimate, exalted status of Jesus Christ, according to Hebrews 1:3 and 13? How is it superior to the position of angels?

> These words we have from Psalm 110. Luther called it the chief of all the Psalms. The first verse, and the fourth about Melchizedek, contain the hidden mysteries, which we never should have understood without the exegesis of the Holy Spirit. It is from this psalm that the expression, which is become one of the great articles of our faith, **sitting at the right hand of God,** has been taken into the New Testament.[1]

There are at least 14 references in the New Testament to Psalm 110:1 stating that Jesus sits at the right hand of God. Five of those references are in Hebrews!

What do you learn about Jesus from Peter's quoting of Psalm 110 in his sermon at Pentecost, in Acts 2:32-36?

The resurrection of Jesus brought about the victory over sin and death. Jesus finished His work on earth and ascended into Heaven, and was given the place of highest honor and exaltation. God the Father, the Majesty on High, seated Jesus His Son at His right hand. Hallelujah!

Jesus' work regarding our salvation is complete, but there is still the anticipation of something more.

What has not yet happened, according to Hebrews 1:13 and 1 Corinthians 15:25?

As we learn more about the recipients of this letter, we will see that they were suffering under persecution (Hebrews 12:4). Realizing that Jesus will put all His enemies under subjection would have been a very reassuring truth.

The writer of the letter to the Hebrews mentions the future often. Note his comments in the verses below.

Hebrews 3:6

Hebrews 3:14

Hebrews 6:11-12

Hebrews 10:25

Hebrews 10:36-37

Hebrews 13:14

Because Jesus is seated at the right hand of God, and exalted, He possesses divine power and authority.

> We are so familiar with this truth, that its infinite magnificence hardly strikes us. God is a God who is, and must be, infinitely jealous of His honor: His glory He will not give to another. When Jesus, the crucified Son of Man, takes His place at the right hand of the Majesty on high, it can only be because He is also the Son of God, because He is God. And it assures us that now the power and dominion of God Himself are in His hands, to carry out the work of redemption to its full consummation, until all His enemies have been put under His feet, and He shall deliver up the kingdom to the Father.[2]

The future is in the hands of Jesus and so are we.

I'd like to close this lesson with one more review of the passage we have been studying. I love how one commentator entitles Hebrews 1:5-14: The Incomparable Majesty of the Eternal, Exalted Son.[3] I am finding that my vocabulary is not adequate to describe and praise Jesus for all that He is.

Using whatever words seem appropriate—simple or eloquent—read Hebrews 1:5-14 and summarize what it tells you about Jesus.

The hymn "Fairest Lord Jesus" has been coming to mind throughout my study. Jesus is fairer, purer, brighter, and dearer than any other.

Fairest Lord Jesus! Ruler of all nature! O Thou of God and man the Son!
Thee will I cherish, Thee will I honor, Thou, my soul's glory, joy, and crown!

Fair are the meadows, fairer still the woodlands, robed in the blooming garb of spring;
Jesus is fairer, Jesus is purer, Who makes the woeful heart to sing!

Fair is the sunshine, fairer still the moonlight, and all the twinkling starry host;
Jesus shines brighter, Jesus shines purer, Than all the angels heav'n can boast!

All fairest beauty, Heavenly and earthly, wondrously, Jesus, is found in Thee;
None can be nearer, fairer, or dearer, than Thou my Savior art to me.

Beautiful Savior! Lord of all the nations! Son of God and Son of Man!
Glory and honor, praise, adoration, now and forevermore be thine.[4]

WARNING – WARNING – WARNING

LESSON 5: THE FIRST WARNING
HEBREWS 2:1-4

Praise the name, the excellent name, of Jesus! We've seen that He is Son, God, and Lord. The writer of Hebrews has brought attention clearly on the person and the work and the exaltation of Jesus Christ. This was to prepare his readers (which include us) for what he would say next. The letter to the Hebrews is a sermon where the writer speaks as a pastor to his people with great concern for their spiritual lives. Some commentators refer to the writer of Hebrews as "the pastor" and I will begin to do so now as well.

After a beautiful and brilliant introduction, the pastor delivers his first warning to his readers. The style of delivery with which he has begun will continue throughout this letter. There will be sections of explanation of biblical truth and sections of exhortation conveying his concern and serious warnings to his readers. So that we will notice the connection between his introduction and his warning, we will begin our study today in Hebrews 1 and continue into Hebrews 2.

Please pray that you will hear and heed the word of the Lord and depend on His Holy Spirit.

Please read Hebrews 1:1–2:4.

What transition word or phrase in Hebrews 2:1 does the pastor use to show us that the superiority of Jesus should affect our response to His word?

The basic warning is given in Hebrews 2:1. Note two aspects – <u>what to do</u> and <u>what not to do</u>.

Consider the all-important message we are to heed. How does the pastor describe it in Hebrews 2:3?

What logic and motivation does the pastor use in Hebrews 2:2 to encourage us toward right behavior?

Now we've got our feet wet! We've waded into the first serious warning from the pastor. It's appropriate to think about water, currents, and boating now because of the choice of words in these verses. We're going to head out into some deeper water as we try to understand this passage. Ready?

Please look up the following words:
Pay attention: Strong's #4337
Greek word:
Greek definition:

This is a nautical technical term, meaning to hold (a ship) toward port. Teodorico suggests that it indicates the fastening of anchors to the sea bed to keep the ship from drifting.[1]

Much / More: Strong's #4056
Greek word:
Greek definition:

Drift away: Strong's #3901
Greek word:
Greek definition:

> The image of a drifting ship, carried by the current beyond a fixed point, furnished a vivid metaphor for the failure to keep a firm grip on the truth through carelessness and lack of concern. The writer warns his readers that they are in danger of losing sight of the reality of Christian salvation.[2]

I wonder if any questions are coming to mind. This is the first of the passages in Hebrews that are difficult to interpret and have various explanations. The first rule of interpretation is to understand what the author intended. We must look at his words and his context and the whole teaching of the Bible as well. And we must be careful to keep our own opinions and assumptions out of the way.

Here are some questions about this passage: 1. Is the pastor speaking to true believers, or false believers (which are actually unbelievers), or unbelievers? 2. If the pastor is speaking to true believers, is he indicating that they can lose their salvation? 3. What is the punishment that he speaks of?

Think about it. After looking at Hebrews 1 and 2 thus far, how would you answer the questions above?

I don't have the wisdom, maturity, and scholarly knowledge to declare that "I have the final answer." I will humbly share my interpretation to the best of my understanding, which is what I will do throughout this study. And if the Lord corrects or enlightens me to a different conclusion, I'll edit this workbook to reflect it!

Let's bring attention to a few details:

Who needs to pay close attention to the word of the Lord? What pronouns are used in Hebrews 2:1-4? What does this indicate?

How is salvation described in Hebrews 2:3-4?

What behavior is to be avoided, according to Hebrews 2:3?

You've just observed the facts that some commentators have highlighted as they interpret this passage to apply to Christian believers. Warren Wiersbe points out that the danger they face is not rejecting the gospel, but neglecting it.[3]

How can you give more abundant attention to the message of the Lord, rather than neglecting it? List some specific examples of what you can do (or perhaps not do) on a regular basis.

We can also notice that the pastor warns of punishment for neglecting so great a salvation. The Greek word he uses literally means "payment of wages" and is better translated as recompense or reward, even though this would be a reward in a negative sense. It is in this book of Hebrews that we will learn more about the discipline of the Lord which is given to correct, teach, and train us in faith and righteousness.

For comparison to another warning similar to that in Hebrews 2:1-4, please read Galatians 1:3-7. Is Paul speaking to Christians?_____ What is his concern?

Paul's letter to the Galatians addresses the church's problem of legalism, rather than neglect. As long as we are in our mortal sin-stained bodies on earth, there will be all kinds of temptations to draw us away from sincere devotion to Christ. I'm thankful for the concern of wise pastors and so thankful for the faithfulness of our Savior and the indwelling Holy Spirit.

How does Ephesians 1:13-14 assure believers of their salvation?

What is our assurance of salvation according to 1 John 5:12-13?

That's good news! Do you believe that Jesus Christ is the Son of God who died for your sins? The pastor to the Hebrews urged his people to pay very close attention to the message of the gospel. He pointed out that Jesus spoke the message Himself.

What was the gospel message that Jesus shared, according to Mark 1:14-15? And John 8:24?

How did Paul summarize the gospel, according to 1 Corinthians 15:2-4?

What did Paul urge believers to do, based on the truth of the gospel, according to Romans 6:9-12?

And how did Paul explain how he lived out the gospel in Galatians 2:20?

Have you believed the gospel? Are you paying very close attention to the gospel? Have you heard that you need to preach the gospel to yourself every day?

The basics of the gospel message are presented below using colors as a way to remember them, which is sometimes called the "wordless book." Use the truths in the references above and below to reflect on the necessity of the gospel. Note what stands out to you the most right now.

*Gold: God is holy and we must be holy to enter Heaven. (1 Peter 1:6)

*Black: Sin separates all mankind from God, and leads to eternal death. (Romans 3:23, 6:23)

*Red: The blood of Christ was shed when He gave His life as a substitute for ours. (Romans 5:8-9)

*White: We are forgiven, purified, and accepted by God when we confess that we sinned, and believe that Jesus died to forgive our sins. (2 Corinthians 5:21, John 1:12)

*Green: We grow in our faith and God transforms us into the image of His Son as we read the Bible, pray, trust, and obey the Lord. (Romans 8:28-29, 2 Peter 3:18)

Let us always pay extra close attention to our great salvation! There are many more blessings of the gospel that we haven't covered in this lesson. God's grace is amazing and unending and necessary every day.

LESSON 6: THE PASTOR'S MESSAGE
OVERVIEW OF HEBREWS

I hope you've enjoyed our first lessons from the book of Hebrews. It's deep, isn't it? Now that you've had a taste of the pastor's message, and a glimpse of his style of writing, I'd like to take some time to get an overview of the whole book. This is often done in a study in the very first lesson, but because the pastor started off with a profound and intriguing introduction about the majesty and superiority of the Son of God, it seemed best to follow his lead and put our attention on Jesus Christ first as well.

With our modern technology today, it's easy to press the pause button on any device, and then pick up right where you left off when you are ready to begin the program or music again. That's what we will do now.

Please pray that you will hear and heed the word of the Lord and receive understanding from the Holy Spirit.

"Who wrote the book of Hebrews?" This is the most common reaction to the mention of the book! Only the Lord knows the answer to that question! Even if we don't know his name, we can still know a little bit about him from his writing. We observed in the last lesson (according to Hebrews 2:3) that he was not an eye-witness of Jesus, but received the gospel message from those who heard Him personally.

What else can we learn about the author of this book, based on the following verses? Briefly note your answers below.

Hebrews 10:34

Hebrews 13:18-19

Hebrews 13:22

Hebrews 13:23

Hebrews 13:24

This sermon, called a "word of exhortation," was from someone who truly cared about the people to whom he was writing. As someone who is writing to others myself, I also desire that those who read my words will be encouraged in their faith and commitment to Jesus. And I hope my words will point you to an intimate and obedient relationship to our Lord. But I don't personally know the circumstances of your lives. This pastor did know the people to whom he was writing. We observed in the last lesson (according to Hebrews 13:22), that he calls them "brothers," which would indicate that they were believers and members of the family of God.

What can we learn about the recipients of this sermon based on the following verses? Briefly note your answers below.

Hebrews 3:1

Hebrews 5:12

Hebrews 6:10

Hebrews 10:25

Hebrews 10:32-34

Hebrews 12:4

Hebrews 13:7

Hebrews 13:9

How would you describe these believers? In what ways, if any, are you similar to them?

Another important characteristic of these believers that will become obvious as we read through the rest of the sermon is that they recognized the authority of the Old Testament and were thoroughly acquainted with the Jewish religion.

> The author assumes his audience has an extensive knowledge of the Old Testament. Of all the writings of the New Testament, none is more saturated with overt references to the Old Testament. The author so filled his discourse with Old Testament thoughts and passages that they permeate every chapter. The writer offers nineteen summaries of Old Testament material, and thirteen times he mentions an Old Testament name or topic, often without reference to a specific context.[1]

The pastor presents the people and events of the Old Testament as real people and actual historical events. It's true! It happened! It was a foreshadowing of the final revelation of God's message to us in His Son. The book of Hebrews shows us how to see Jesus throughout all of Scripture and how to follow—or not follow—the examples of the people.

Let's check out some of these Old Testament topics. Note the word or phrase mentioned in the verses below. I've given you the references in case you are interested in further study.

Hebrews 2:16 - He gives aid to _____. (Genesis 22:18)

Hebrews 3:2 - _____ was faithful. (Numbers 12:7)

Hebrews 3:8 - Do not harden your hearts as in the _____, in the day of trial in the _____. (Deuteronomy 9:22-24)

Hebrews 4:4 - And God rested _____. (Genesis 2:1-2)

Hebrews 6:20 - Jesus, _____ forever according to the order of _____. (Genesis 14:18-20)

Hebrews 7:14 - Our Lord was descended from _____, and about that _____ _____. (Genesis 49:10 and 28; Numbers 3:10-12)

Hebrews 8:5 - Moses was divinely instructed when he was about to make the _____. (Exodus 39:32)

Hebrews 9:1-3 - The first _____ had regulations of divine service and the earthly sanctuary. For a _____ was prepared, the outer one in which were the _____, the _____, and the _____; this is called _____. Behind the second _____, there was a second section called _____. (Exodus 40:18-29)

Hebrews 9:19 - When every _____ had been proclaimed by Moses to all the people according to the _____, he took the _____, with _____, _____, and _____, and sprinkled both the scroll itself and all the people. (Exodus 24:5-8)

Hebrews 10:11 - Every priest stands ministering daily and _____ repeatedly the same _____, which can never take away sins. (Exodus 29:38-42; Leviticus 4:28-29, 35)

Hebrews 11:32 - Time is too short for me to tell of _____ and _____ and _____ and _____, also of _____ and _____ and the prophets. (Judges 6:11-7:24; Judges 4:6-24; Judges 13:24-16:31; Judges 11:1-12:7; 1 Samuel 16:13-17:50)

Hebrews 12:22 - But you have come to _____, the _____, the heavenly _____, to myriads of angels in festive gathering. (Psalm 132:13-14; Psalm 48:2; Deuteronomy 33:2; Daniel 7:10)

Hebrews 13:20-21 - Now may the God of peace who brought again from the dead our Lord Jesus, the great Shepherd of the sheep, by _____, equip you with everything good to do His will. (Psalm 23:1; Isaiah 55:3; Zechariah 9:11)

If this is unfamiliar territory for you, don't worry. We will learn more about these topics as we come to them throughout our study.

Why did the pastor spend so much time referring to these Old Testament concepts? Most commentators have concluded that he was concerned that the believers who were going through difficult times were considering returning to the Jewish religion.

> The temple was still standing when this book was written, and all the priestly ceremonies were still being carried on daily. How easy it would have been for these Jewish believers to escape persecution by going back into the old Mosaic system that they had known before.[2]

Not only will the pastor explain that Jesus Christ is the fulfillment of all that was commanded and promised in the Old Testament, but he will also show that the blessings received from the great salvation of Jesus are exceedingly and eternally better than the previous ones.

What is better and why (if mentioned), according to the following verses?

Hebrews 7:19

Hebrews 7:22-24

Hebrews 9:23-24

Hebrews 11:39-40

My summary of the teachings above is: Jesus is better! It doesn't matter what I compare Him to—Jesus is better.

Can you say that too? List a few things about which you can say: "Jesus is better than...."

As we have looked at the overview of this book, have you noticed that I haven't mentioned an outline? I like it when there is a structure, a plan to go by as we follow the development of ideas. But alas, one of the mysteries of this sermon is its structure. Every commentary that I've looked at has a different outline.

And yet, the pastor's writing is brilliant. Those who understand ancient Greek have noted that his use of the language is the best of the New Testament authors. Hebrews 1:1 has been called "the most perfect Greek sentence in the New Testament." [3] *This pastor was highly educated, based on his excellent use of logic and rhetoric and word choices.*

> Hebrews does not develop in a neat outline from point A to point Z. Rather, the author switches back and forth between exposition and exhortation. Although the two work together powerfully, weaving a tapestry of concepts toward the accomplishment of his purpose, they contribute to that purpose in different manners.[4]

I think the easiest structure for us to grasp will be to highlight the five specific warnings given in the midst of the pastor's (sometimes lengthy) exhortations. Then as we study the book, we will notice how he weaves his explanations and exhortations together to prompt us to faithfulness to the word of the Lord and hope in His promises.

Please briefly note the five warnings in the verses below:

#1: Hebrews 2:1

#2: Hebrews 3:12-13

#3: Hebrews 6:11-12

#4: Hebrews 10:25-26; 35-36

#5: Hebrews 12:25

These verses are found in the midst of very serious admonitions and just as we noted when studying Hebrews 2:1-4, there is difficulty and disagreement in interpreting them.

Warren Wiersbe (1929-2019), a pastor himself, said that each passage is best understood as an encouragement to heed God's Word, and the pastor to the Hebrews points out the sad spiritual consequences that result if we do not do so.[5]

Here is Wiersbe's description of these passages:

> **Drifting** from the Word – Hebrews 2:1-4 (due to neglect)
> **Doubting** the Word – Hebrews 3:7-4:13 (due to a hard heart and unbelief)
> **Dullness** toward the Word – Hebrews 5:11-6:20 (due to sluggishness)
> **Despising** the Word – Hebrews 10:26-39 (due to willful disobedience)
> **Defying** the Word – Hebrews 12:14-29 (due to a refusal to hear)

One thing leads to another! It's a terrible downward spiral that will result in the discipline of the Lord. I'd rather walk in obedience, fellowship, and blessing, wouldn't you?

We should go ahead and examine our hearts, minds, and ears right now. Are any of the verses that you noted above (or categories from Pastor Wiersbe) encouraging you to make a change in some way? If so, how?

This has been somewhat of a long lesson. May it serve to help us as we move forward, not only in our study but in our walk with the Lord.

LESSON 7: Jesus Christ — The Son of Man
Hebrews 2:5-9

It's time to return to our regularly scheduled exposition on Jesus Christ. We actually paused at the perfect moment in our study. The pastor introduced his sermon with a focus on the exalted majesty and deity of Jesus, the Son of God; then he gave us the warning to pay attention to His message; now he will transition to point out that the Son of God became the Son of Man.

Please pray that you will trust the Holy Spirit to give you understanding of the word of God.

Please read Hebrews 1:13-2:9, then re-read Hebrews 2:5-9.

Even though Hebrews 2:5-9 is about Jesus, you might notice that angels have been mentioned again. What do we need to realize about angels, based on verses 5, 7, and 8?

Hebrews 2:6-8 includes a quote from Psalm 8:4-6. Most versions of the Bible have translated Psalm 8:5: "for a little while lower than the angels." (NKJV and NLT do not use this translation.) What do these verses in Hebrews tell you about Jesus?

What statements in Hebrews 2:5-9 are related to Hebrews 1:13, "Sit at my right hand until I make your enemies a footstool for your feet?"

The pastor chose Scripture that testifies to the humanity and the deity of Jesus Christ. It encompasses the incarnation (becoming a man) and the exaltation (receiving glory and honor) of the Son. He also explains that God the Father has put everything in subjection to Him, but based on Psalm 110:1, "until I make Your enemies Your footstool," we are still waiting for the final fulfillment of this promise. "At present, we do not see everything in subjection to Him." (Hebrews 2:8)

Throughout this sermon, the pastor will be encouraging the believers to persevere through the difficult times, to hope and trust in Jesus, because one day they will see all of His enemies conquered.

How does the truth that, in the future, we will see the enemies of Christ subjugated under His feet, encourage you today?

For the very first time, we see the pastor use the name of our Lord. What is shown to be of great importance in Hebrews 2:9? What brought about the crowning with glory?

In the Greek, the proper name Jesus is placed at the end of the clause, for the element of surprise as well as emphasis.[1] The pastor will do this each time he brings attention to Jesus. The pre-existing, pre-eminent Son of God became the Son of Man, a human, one of us. His pre-incarnate glory was incredible, but the pastor is teaching us that His obedient life and suffering in death brought about an even greater splendor. Wow. Taking on flesh did not make Jesus inferior to angels.

This is personal. According to Hebrews 2:9, why did Jesus suffer and die?

Please note ways that Jesus suffered, based on Matthew 27:22-31.

How does Romans 5:8-9 explain Jesus' death?

Please read the next passage, Hebrews 2:10-18, where the pastor further explains the significance of Jesus' suffering. What reasons for His suffering are given in Hebrews 2:14, 17 and 18?

> Hebrews 2:5-18 completes the description of the eternal, exalted Son in 1:5-14 by showing how His incarnation and suffering were the means to His exaltation as all-sufficient Savior.[2]

Philippians 2:5-11 also beautifully declares the deity, incarnation, and exaltation of Jesus. Read this passage and note the similarities to Hebrews 2:5-9.

What did Jesus Himself say to the men on the road to Emmaus after His resurrection, in Luke 24:25-27?

Jesus took on our nature, suffered and died for us, saved us from God's wrath, all in accordance with the Scriptures. And it was all planned by the grace of God. The pastor certainly understood the grace of God, but he doesn't refer to it in his sermon very often.

Let's make sure we are amazed by God's great grace.

How does John 1:14 describe Jesus?

What do Romans 5:15 and Romans 5:20 tell you about grace?

Describe what happened because of grace, according to 2 Corinthians 8:9?

What does Ephesians 2:8-9 tell us about God's grace and our salvation?

The all-sufficient, super-abundant, never-ending grace of our God and our Savior Jesus Christ changes our lives. It rescues us and keeps us. It was terrible, painful, and costly for Jesus. How great is the grace of God!

Please read Hebrews 2:5-9 once more. What is the most meaningful part of this passage to you?

But we see Jesus. He is crowned with glory because He suffered and died for you. And me. Praise the name of Jesus.

LESSON 8: Jesus Christ — Made like Us
Hebrews 2:10-18

While we have already studied passages that tell us of the honor and glory of Jesus Christ, we are about to consider another that communicates love and sacrifice from both God the Father and God the Son who became man.

Please pray that you will trust the Holy Spirit to give you understanding of the precious truths of the word of God.

Please read Hebrews 2:10-18.

How is God the Father described in Hebrews 2:10?

What was God's plan according to Hebrews 2:10?

Consider John 3:16 along with Hebrews 2:10. Why did God carry out this plan and what was His sacrifice through it?

Some of you might wonder if there was some imperfection in Jesus which necessitated Him being made "perfect through suffering." Oh, no, there was absolutely no imperfection in Him. We have grasped that truth from the opening statements of Hebrew 1. "Perfect" means complete, effective, and its use here indicates that Jesus accomplished God's plan through suffering.

What title is given to Jesus in Hebrews 2:10?

The pastor used a special word that has been translated differently in many versions of the Bible.

> **Archegos** is (1) one who goes first on the path; hence leader, prince, pioneer (Heb. 2:10); (2) one who causes something to begin, originator, founder, initiator (Heb.12:2).[1] The Greek word archegos translated pioneer is used of a "prince" or leader, the representative head of a family. It also carries nuances of "trailblazer," one who breaks through to new ground for those who follow him. It is used some thirty-five times in the Greek OT and four times in the NT, always of Christ (Acts 3:15; 5:31; Heb. 2:10; 12:2).[2]

What did Jesus do that made Him a trailblazer, according to Hebrews 2:10-18?

We could do nothing to help ourselves. And Jesus came to our rescue.

Perhaps you've heard Paul Harvey's story of the man who discovered birds trying to find shelter during a heavy snowfall. After many attempts to entice them into his warm, lighted barn he thought to himself: "If only I could be a bird, and mingle with them and speak their language. Then I could tell them not to be afraid. Then I could show them the way to the safe warm barn. But I would have to be one of them so they could see and hear and understand."[3]

The incarnation and suffering of Jesus Christ are emphasized in the passage we are studying. He became one of us.

How is Jesus like us (humankind in general), according to Hebrews 2:11-18?

Do the three Old Testament quotations seem a little bit unusual to you? They show the close association and intimate relationship that Jesus has with us. When we look at the context of the quotes in the Old Testament, we'll see that they come from messianic passages which refer to the suffering of our Savior.

I've quoted the passage and indented the Old Testament references on the next page.

Circle the words or phrases in the passage that show Jesus' association with humankind, then summarize how the Old Testament passage refers to Jesus.

^NIV^ **Hebrews 2:11-13** Both the One who makes men holy and those who are made holy are of the same family. So Jesus is not ashamed to call them brothers.

^12^ He says,

> "I will declare Your name to my brothers; in the presence of the congregation I will sing Your praises." See Psalm 22:22 and Psalm 22:14-22.

^13^ And again,

> "I will put my trust in Him." See Isaiah 8:17, and Psalm 22:4-8.

And again He says,

> "Here am I, and the children God has given me." See Isaiah 8:14, 18.

What do you think about the Son of God becoming the Son of Man and identifying Himself so intimately with us? How does this impact you personally?

What weaknesses, fears, and needs are given as reasons for Jesus becoming like us, according to Hebrews 2:14-18?

Let's think about the exciting victory that Jesus has already won because He became one of us. Wiersbe says: "Satan uses the fear of death as a terrible weapon to gain control over the lives of people."[4] *That's the bondage the pastor refers to in Hebrews 2:15.*

What did Jesus do by becoming a man, according to Hebrews 2:15?

Please look up the definition of the following word:
Destroy: Strong's #2673
Greek word:
Greek definition:

What did Jesus do according to 1 Corinthians 15:20-26?

How do these scriptures inform your thoughts about your own death?

Just a little side note here . . . the pastor has been showing that Jesus is better than the angels through many comparisons. Jesus is a better Savior than any angel ever could be because angels cannot die. Jesus did what we would have thought impossible: He, God the Son, became a man. God in the flesh. A mystery and a miracle. I am overwhelmed with this truth every time I think about it. And even more inconceivable—God the Son, in the flesh, died.

What is your reaction to the incredible topics we've just considered? Reflect on: Jesus becoming one of us; Jesus destroying the devil; Jesus suffering and dying.

Whatever you may be experiencing right now, Jesus has experienced in one way or another.

What phrase tells us this in Hebrews 2:17?

What title is given to Jesus in Hebrews 2:17? (Include the adjectives.)

Why was Jesus given this role according to Hebrews 2:17?

What is the result of His experiences according to Hebrews 2:18?

The next sentence from the pastor is a fervent plea based on everything he has said thus far.

To whom does the pastor speak in Hebrews 3:1?

What does he urge his readers to do in Hebrews 3:1?

Let's follow those instructions! Every day! And right now.

Please read Hebrews 2:1-18, and consider our great Savior Jesus. We've studied the entire chapter. For review, please list all the descriptions of Jesus. Let this be a time of prayer, worship, adoration, and thankfulness.

LESSON 9: THE GREATEST OF ALL TIME
HEBREWS 3:1-6

The greatest of all time is not the best athlete, or the winner of the Nobel Peace Prize, or even your own mother! No matter who you respect the most, the greatest of all time is Jesus!

I'm excited about considering even more of the greatness of Jesus. The pastor described what our Savior gave us as "so great a salvation" in Hebrews 2:3. Why is it so great? Because of the greatness of the One who made it possible.

In Judaism, Moses is considered the greatest of all the prophets. So, it's time for a comparison between Jesus and Moses.

Please pray that you will hear and heed the Word of God and trust the Holy Spirit to give you His perspective.

^{NAS} **Hebrews 3:1** Therefore, holy brethren, partakers of a heavenly calling, consider Jesus, the Apostle and High Priest of our confession. He was faithful to Him who appointed Him, as Moses also was in all His house.

What roles were given to Jesus and how did He receive them?

Please look up the definition of the following word:
Apostle: Strong's #652
Greek word:
Greek definition:

I'm used to the 12 disciples being called apostles because they were messengers sent by Jesus to preach the gospel. But I'm learning something new here. The pastor calls Jesus "the Apostle" when comparing Him to Moses because Moses was a messenger sent by God. The Greek verb "apostellein," to send, is used often of Moses.

Look at Exodus 3:15 and 4:28, and note who sent Moses and what he was sent to do.

An apostle is one who is sent with full authority for a particular mission. He is a messenger. If we keep these points in mind, we will also understand that the pastor is still emphasizing that we must listen to the message given by Jesus.

Just for a reminder, what did the pastor warn us about in Hebrews 2:1-4?

In our last lesson, we were introduced to Jesus' role as High Priest. We need to learn a little bit about it now and in later lessons, we will learn much more from the pastor regarding this role.

How did God set up the priesthood according to Exodus 40:1-16? Briefly summarize what Moses' role was.

The Jewish Encyclopedia gives us details about the responsibilities of the High Priest. They are noted below.

Underline the activities that only the High Priest could carry out.

> The distinguished rank of the high priest: On the Day of Atonement he alone entered the Holy of Holies, to make atonement for his house and for the people (Lev. 16); on that occasion he wore white linen garments instead of his ordinary and more costly vestments. He alone could offer the sacrifices for the sins of the priests, or of the people, or of himself (Lev. 4); and only he could officiate at the sacrifices following his own or another priest's consecration (Lev. 9). He also offered a meal-offering every morning and evening for himself and the whole body of the priesthood (Lev. 6:14-15).[1]

According to Psalm 99:6, Moses and Aaron were both priests and called on the name of the Lord. But Moses was never the High Priest. That special role belonged to his brother Aaron. Moses was, however, greatly revered by all Jewish people, because the entire system of the Jewish religion—including the law and the practice of worship—came through Moses.

The pastor explains that Jesus is superior to Moses.

Please read Hebrews 3:1-6, then note the comparisons between Jesus and Moses in the chart below.

Jesus	Moses

Moses is a great guy! He was faithful to the Lord. But Jesus is greater! The message of salvation given through Jesus is what the pastor wanted his people to believe in and hold on to.

Is there someone that you admire and listen to more than you listen to Jesus? Is there someone who influences you and could cause you to neglect the truth from Jesus? Please evaluate books, articles, music, TV, friends, family, and traditions.

> Even those that are holy brethren, and partakers of the heavenly calling, have need to stir up one another to think more of Christ than they do, to have Him more in their minds; the best of His people think too seldom and too slightly of Him. We must consider Christ as He is described to us in the scriptures, and form our apprehensions of him thence, not from any vain conceptions and fancies of our own.[2]

How often do you think about Jesus? What do you think about Him? What passages of Scripture about Him do you hold dear?

While the pastor shows us that Jesus is greater than Moses, he also highlights faithfulness in this passage. He begins to emphasize the critical need for faith, which he will discuss repeatedly in the rest of his sermon.

Please circle every mention of faithfulness below.

^{NIV} **Hebrews 3:1** Therefore, holy brothers, who share in the heavenly calling, fix your thoughts on Jesus, the Apostle and High Priest whom we confess. ²He was faithful to the One who appointed Him, just as Moses was faithful in all God's house. ³Jesus has been found worthy of greater honor than Moses, just as the builder of a house has greater honor than the house itself. ⁴For every house is built by someone, but God is the builder of everything. ⁵Moses was faithful as a servant in all God's house, testifying to what would be said in the future. ⁶But Christ is faithful as a Son over God's house. And we are His house, if we hold on to our courage and the hope of which we boast.

You might be wondering about the mention of God's house. There are several Old Testament references which are alluded to here.

What promise was made by God to the priest Eli in 1 Samuel 2:35?

What promise was made by God to King David in 1 Chronicles 17:14?

How is the "house" described in Hebrews 3:1-6? (You might want to underline each phrase where it is mentioned.)

The pastor is reminding his readers that they became the house of God, members of His family, through their faith in Jesus Christ. They prove that they belong to God if they hold on to Him.

Let's think about two compelling instructions that the pastor urges us to heed.

Highlight the instruction in the verses below and look up the corresponding words.

^{NAS} **Hebrews 3:1** Holy brethren, partakers of the heavenly calling, consider the Apostle and High Priest of our confession — Jesus.

Consider: Strong's #2657
Greek word:
Greek definition:

^{ESV} **Hebrews 3:6** But Christ is faithful over God's house as a Son. And we are His house if indeed we hold fast our confidence and our boasting in our hope.

Hold: Strong's #2722
Greek word:
Greek definition:

The pastor urged the believers to whom he was writing to think very carefully about the greatest Messenger and greatest High Priest. Not Moses. But Jesus. And the pastor urged these believers to actively engage in keeping their faith in Him, by holding on to their confidence in Jesus. He previously used a nautical term to warn them not to drift away. "Hold fast", the Greek word katecho, is also a nautical term meaning "to hold one's course toward, head for, steer for." ³

If you don't want to go adrift, you'll have to keep a close eye on your heading. The heading is the direction in which a vessel's bow points. A ship, a sailboat, or a canoe will float off course if attention isn't given to the navigation.

How can you follow the exhortation of the pastor to consider Jesus and hold fast to the confidence we have in Him?

    What attitudes are important?

What actions are necessary?

Are there any adjustments you need to make so that you don't drift off course?

Remember, the pastor wants to encourage his readers to continue in their Christian faith. He's shown the positive examples of Jesus and Moses, and next will show how bad things get when people are disobedient to the Lord.

I want to follow the good examples!

WARNING — WARNING — WARNING

LESSON 10: Beware of Unbelief: The Second Warning
Hebrews 3:7-19

Brace yourself! A blast from the past is going to sound a loud warning signal to believers today! We should receive this warning as one given by our loving Heavenly Father who wants us to believe in all He has said to us through His Son. A warning is a gracious gift to help us, to bring attention to possible problems, and to help us make corrections before it's too late.

Please pray that you will obey the Holy Spirit as He gives you guidance today.

Please read Hebrews 3:1-19. Verses 1-6 are examples of the faithfulness of Jesus and Moses, and verses 7-19 are examples of the unfaithfulness of the Israelites in the wilderness.

Hebrews 3:7-11 includes a quote from Psalm 95:7-11. How does the pastor refer to the passage? What does this tell you about the Bible?

It might seem to be off-topic to highlight the fact that the Holy Spirit speaks to us through the words of the Scriptures. But, if we want to heed the message of Jesus, and think carefully about our High Priest Jesus, and hold on to the teachings of the Lord, we need to know how to hear Him!

The Holy Spirit speaks through the Bible. There are religions and spiritual practices that instruct you to empty your mind so that you can hear something spiritual. Don't do that! Fill your mind and your thoughts with the words of the Bible so that you will hear the Holy Spirit.

What did the Israelites do in the wilderness that resulted in sin? Note their behavior in the chart below:

According to Hebrews 3:7-11	**According to Hebrews 3:15-19**

*This is a serious warning. The Israelites **heard** the words of the Lord and rebelled. They didn't believe His words. They didn't trust Him to deliver them through the hardships of the desert. They didn't trust the power of the Lord to conquer the giants in their promised land.*

How does Hebrews 3:12 summarize the behavior of the Israelites? (We'll come back to the exhortation to believers soon.)

What were the consequences of the Israelites unbelief, according to Hebrews 3:8-11 and 15-19?

The pastor has presented a group of people (except for Moses, Joshua, and Caleb) who were unfaithful to their God and they were disciplined. They weren't allowed to enter the Promised Land, the place of rest from their wanderings.

The behavior of the Israelites in the wilderness is such a sobering example for us as believers today. They had the word of the Lord given directly to Moses; they saw the pillar of cloud by day and fire by night as the tangible presence of God. They received the miracle of manna every day! And they experienced so many other evidences of the power of God.

And yet they didn't hold fast to their faith in Him.

> "To fall away from the living God" is to act in such a way that one definitively rejects the reality of His power and the validity of His promises.[1]

In Hebrews 3:12-13:

What is the pastor's warning?

What is the pastor's instruction?

> **Lest any of you be hardened.** This phrase is a passive of permission: "Lest any of you allow yourselves to be hardened." He says in effect, "Don't let the powerful opposition of the society around you, or the rewards it would give for conformity, blind you to the reality of God's power and the certainty of His promise so that you abandon Him for temporal reward."[2]

Are you facing opposition from those around you? Is there pressure to conform to beliefs and behaviors of the world?

Note the exhortations which are similar to Hebrews 3:12-13, given by these other faithful followers of Christ:
Paul - Romans 12:2

Ephesians 4:22

1 Timothy 6:10-12

Peter - 1 Peter 1:13-15

John - 1 John 2:15

Before moving on to the next verse where the pastor encourages his readers to persevere, we need to look at one more very difficult concept in the warning of Hebrews 3:12. In the Greek, "departing" is the word "apostenai" which gives us the word apostasy. It means to fall away, desert,[2] depart from, and repudiate one's position.[3]

This word grieves me terribly. The common concept of apostasy is that it refers to someone who becomes a Christian and then later rejects Christ and His salvation. But as Scripture points out, when we trust in Jesus Christ as our Savior, we have the guarantee of our salvation through the indwelling Holy Spirit (Ephesians 1:13-14).

What is apostasy then? Can someone say they believe in Jesus for salvation and then reject His salvation? This question has been debated for centuries. I will share my understanding based on several Scriptures.

Jesus pointed out in the Sermon on the Mount that some who make claims that they know Jesus do not truly belong to Him. What do they say, and what does Jesus say, according to Matthew 7:21-23?

The word "apostenai" is used in Luke 8:13 and translated as "fall away." What does this verse tell us?

Why does Paul say that apostasy will happen, according to 1 Timothy 4:1?

What does 1 John 2:19 say?

The pastor of the Hebrews has given his readers an opportunity to examine their hearts. What do they believe? My understanding of apostasy is that a person who thinks that he or she is a Christian and then rejects the truths of the Christian faith, was never truly a Christian.

And so, I suggest that "falling away from the faith" is a very misleading phrase. It's a little wordy, but I'd like to define apostasy as "falling away from the concepts that sounded good to them at one point in time." Put another way: "deliberately spurning the truths of the gospel."

What is a real Christian? What has happened to them according to Titus 3:3-7? (Note their past, present, and future.)

What change does Ephesians 2:5 say happened to us?

How does the Old Testament describe this change in a person, according to Ezekiel 36:26-27?

Please summarize the result of believing in Christ as your Savior from sin.

Based on what we've seen in the verses above, do you think a person can reject their faith and lose their salvation?

How does the pastor encourage perseverance in our faith in Christ according to Hebrews 3:14?

*This verse must be understood based on the realities of salvation that we considered in the previous passages. It does not teach us that we will be saved **because** we hold on to what we believe. Instead, when we hold on to what we believe, it proves that we have been saved. And once again the Greek word, katecho, is used which was in Hebrews 3:6; katecho tells us to hold one's course steady.*

The pastor describes believers as partakers in Christ according to the NAS and NKJV. Other versions say we are partners or companions of Christ, or that we are sharers in Christ.

We looked at what happens when a person trusts Christ for salvation. And now, let's look at more of the exciting blessings that we receive in Christ! All that Christ gives us is ours now.

What benefits are provided by Jesus to be enjoyed by those who have faith in Him?

Hebrews 2:10

Hebrews 2:11

Hebrews 3:1

Hebrews 4:16

Hebrews 6:4

Hebrews 9:14

We have such a great salvation! We have an intimate relationship with the greatest of all time— Jesus. We have become members of His family and have an open door into our Father God's throne room. I hope you realize that there are so many more blessings that we have received than what we have looked at in the few verses above. And the inheritance that we will receive, that which awaits us in heaven, is beyond our comprehension.

All this is ours if we heed the warnings.

How does the pastor tell us to help each other persevere? Encourage one another daily.

Take a moment to pray for one, or some, of your brothers and sisters in Christ. And then connect with them to encourage them!

^{NKJ} **Ephesians 1:3** Blessed be the God and Father of our Lord Jesus Christ, who has blessed us with every spiritual blessing in the heavenly places in Christ.

LESSON 11: A SABBATH CELEBRATION
Hebrews 4:1-11

Is there no rest for the weary? Oh, yes, there is. Jesus said: "Come to Me, all you who are weary and burdened and I will give you rest" (Matthew 11:28).

Holding on to the message from Jesus will continue to be the theme of the next passage we study. The pastor is still explaining the behavior of the Israelites in the wilderness, who, because of their unbelief, did not enter into God's rest.

Please pray that you will hear and heed the Word of God and trust the Holy Spirit to give you understanding of these precious truths.

We've been studying small sections of the sermon in the last 2 lessons, but Hebrews 3:7-4:13 is a complete unit. It is basically a commentary on Psalm 95:7-11, which the pastor uses to urge his readers to hold on to the message of salvation given through Jesus. That message guarantees rest.

Please read the passage below and highlight each phrase which includes the word "rest" or "enter."

ᴱˢⱽ **Hebrews 3:7-4:13** Therefore, as the Holy Spirit says, "Today, if you hear his voice, ⁸do not harden your hearts as in the rebellion, on the day of testing in the wilderness, ⁹where your fathers put me to the test and saw my works ¹⁰for forty years. Therefore I was provoked with that generation, and said, 'They always go astray in their heart; they have not known my ways.' ¹¹As I swore in my wrath, 'They shall not enter my rest.'" ¹²Take care, brothers, lest there be in any of you an evil, unbelieving heart, leading you to fall away from the living God. ¹³But exhort one another every day, as long as it is called "today," that none of you may be hardened by the deceitfulness of sin. ¹⁴For we share in Christ, if indeed we hold our original confidence firm to the end. ¹⁵As it is said, "Today, if you hear his voice, do not harden your hearts as in the rebellion." ¹⁶For who were those who heard and yet rebelled? Was it not all those who left Egypt led by Moses? ¹⁷And with whom was he provoked for forty years? Was it not with those who sinned, whose bodies fell in the wilderness? ¹⁸And to whom did he swear that they would not enter his rest, but to those who were disobedient? ¹⁹So we see that they were unable to enter because of unbelief. **Hebrews 4:1** Therefore, while the promise of entering his rest still stands, let us fear lest any of you should seem to have failed to reach it. ²For good news came to us just as to them, but the message they heard did not benefit them, because they were not united by faith with those who listened. ³For we who have believed enter that rest, as he has said, "As I swore in my wrath, 'They shall not enter my rest,'" although his works were finished from the foundation of the world. ⁴For he has somewhere spoken of the seventh day in this way: "And God rested on the seventh day from all his works." ⁵And again in this passage he said, "They shall not enter my rest." ⁶Since therefore it remains for some to enter it, and those who formerly received the good news failed to enter because of disobedience, ⁷again he appoints a certain day, "Today," saying through David so long afterward, in the words already quoted, "Today, if you hear his voice, do not harden your hearts." ⁸For if Joshua had given them rest, God would not have spoken of another day later on. ⁹So then, there remains a Sabbath rest for the people of God, ¹⁰for whoever has entered God's rest has also rested from his works as God did from his. ¹¹Let us therefore strive to enter that rest, so that no one may fall by the same sort of disobedience. ¹²For the word of God is living and active, sharper than any two-edged sword, piercing to the division of soul and of spirit, of joints and of marrow, and discerning the thoughts and intentions of the heart. ¹³And no creature is hidden from his sight, but all are naked and exposed to the eyes of him to whom we must give account.

What positive statement does Hebrews 4:1 give us about the promise of God's rest?

And what is the warning that the pastor makes, in Hebrews 4:1 and 4:11?

The good news is that God still offers His rest! We'll see how the pastor makes that important point as we study the passage further. And hopefully, the warning will prompt us to persevere in our faith. There is a blessing now and a great celebration ahead for those who hold on to Jesus.

Please read Numbers 14:1-11, then explain to whom or what the bracketed phrases below are referring.

ᴱˢⱽ **Hebrews 4:2** For good news came to us just as to [them] _____
but [the message they heard] _____
did not benefit them, because they were [not united by faith] _____
with [those who listened.] _____

Just to make sure we understand the point, what was the problem with the Israelites in the wilderness (except for Moses, Joshua, and Caleb)? Look at Hebrews 3:12, 19 and 4:2, 6.

You might know one of the key verses from the book of Hebrews tells us something about faith. What truths do Hebrews 11:1 and 6 give us?

Looking at Hebrews 4:3, what do we see that belief (faith) gives us?

The pastor continues to quote Scriptures as the very spoken words of God (Hebrews 4:4,7), even when they were written by men. He tells us that God's works were finished from the foundation of the world and His rest has been available since that time!

So, God's rest was available to the Israelites, but because of their unbelieving hearts, God refused to let them enter in to it. But did that make God's rest unavailable from that time on?

In Hebrews 4:6-8, how does the pastor explain that God's rest is still available?

A quick note about Joshua—he is another highly regarded Israelite. But as impressive as his fighting at Jericho was, and crossing the Jordan to enter the Promised Land, he still is not as great as Jesus. The matchless excellence of Jesus shines through the whole book of Hebrews.

The Greek word "katapausis" has been used in verses 1-8 for "rest." It means "ceasing from one's work or activity." Sounds good! But something even better is referred to in verse 9.

What very good news is stated in Hebrews 4:9? (The NKJV and NLT do not have the full translation of the Greek word used.)

The Greek word in verse 9 is "sabbatismos." I like this word!

> [The use of sabbatismos] is meant to define more precisely the character of the future rest promised to the people of God. The deliberate choice of this word must have been dictated by the fact that it conveyed a nuance not found in "katapausis."
>
> The term "sabbatismos" stresses the special aspect of festivity and joy, expressed in the adoration and praise of God. The term received its particular nuance from the Sabbath instruction that developed in Judaism on the basis of Exodus 20:8-10, where it was emphasized that rest and praise belong together.[1]

"Faith brings into the present the reality of that which is future, unseen, or heavenly. For that reason, those who have believed can be said to enter God's rest already." [2]

Let's have some Sabbath celebration!

Praise God as you note the truths in the references below:

Ephesians 2:8-9

2 Timothy 1:9

Hebrews 4:10

God our Father and Jesus our Savior have done all the work. It is finished. We can receive rescue and rest by believing their message to us. I am truly relieved because there was no way that I could bring myself from death to life. There was no way that I could pay the debt I owed due to my sin. There was no way that I could do enough good things to make myself acceptable in God's sight. Jesus died and rose again. Paid my debt with His blood. Obeyed every command and resisted every temptation and loved sacrificially.

What's your story? Are you trying to work your way to heaven? Or are you rejoicing in receiving rest? What about this world are you most looking forward to resting from in heaven?

Does it seem strange that the pastor encourages us to strive to enter God's rest? He has pointed out that the key to entering rest is belief. I think the way the disciple John puts it might help us.

What does John 6:29 say?

Keep doing that kind of work, and you'll never get tired of it!

I think you'll be surprised, as I was, to see that the last verses in this passage are tightly connected to the example of the Israelites, even while they are an exhortation to believers today.

What warning is given in Hebrews 4:11-13?

> Those who remain insensitive to the voice of God in Scripture may discover that God's word is also a lethal weapon. When the past generation sought to [disregard] the oath of God and to enter Canaan, they were driven back and fell by the sword of the Amalekites and the Canaanites (Numbers 14:43-45). The word of God poses a judgment that is more threatening and sharper than any double-edged sword because it exposes the intentions of the heart and renders one defenseless before God's scrutinizing gaze.[3]

The warning is also an encouragement. The Word of God shows us when we are truly resting in the work of Christ. It discerns the attitude of our hearts and shows us whether we are believing in Christ alone or not. Let's rest in the Lord and we will learn more about the living Word of God in our next lesson.

LESSON 12: GOD HAS SPOKEN
HEBREWS 4:12-13

*The B – I – B – L – E, yes, that's the book for me! I stand alone on the Word of God, the B – I – B – L – E! The Bible! I love God's word. I love **the** Bible, and I love **my** Bibles. My Bible story is at the beginning of this workbook. But what is God's Bible story? In this lesson, we'll look at key statements that the Bible makes about itself, which is to say—as the pastor in Hebrews says it—what God has said about His own words.*

Please pray that you will hear the Word of God spoken by the Holy Spirit, believe the Word of God, and love the Word of God.

We noticed at the end of the last lesson that Hebrews 4:12-13 is actually a warning and a conclusion to the exhortation to believe God's message. The way the verse begins, "for the word of God...," with the connecting word "for," indicates that the statement is connected to the previous one.

We are accountable to what God has spoken to us. Why? List each description of the Word of God in Hebrews 4:12 in the blanks below, and then note the corresponding truths from the cross-references.

1. _____ 1 Peter 1:23

2. _____ Isaiah 55:11

3. _____ Ephesians 6:17

4 _____ Acts 2:37

5. _____ Jeremiah 17:10

What is the situation for every person on earth, according to Hebrews 4:13? List each phrase, then note the corresponding truths from the cross-references.

1. _____ Proverbs 15:3

2. _____ Psalm 33:13

3. _____ John 12:48

God's Word is the "voice of God" that we should hear, believe, and obey, is it not? This is what the pastor emphasizes in his sermon.

And just for a quick reminder, how has God spoken His word to us, according to Hebrews 1:1-2?

When you stop to think about it, isn't it absolutely amazing that God, the transcendent, self-sufficient, holy One, has communicated His thoughts and ways and love to us?

What is your reaction to the fact that God has spoken and still speaks to us through His Word?

Let's consider some facts about the Scriptures. This is Bibliology 101.

The Bible is inspired by God. *It is the perfectly written result of the direct act of God, through the Holy Spirit, on the human author.[1]*

How does 2 Timothy 3:16 express this?

Jesus affirmed the verbal and plenary inspiration of the Bible. *Verbal inspiration means that every word is inspired; plenary inspiration means that all the words are inspired.[2]*

How does Jesus express the perfection of the Scriptures in Matthew 5:17-18?

The Bible accurately reveals and clearly communicates God's message. *This is called the perspicuity of Scripture, meaning that it is clear and can be understood. The Bible is a plain book. It's simple – it can be understood.[3]*

Scripture describes itself this way! What does Psalm 119:130 say?

Hopefully, the principle of perspicuity will encourage you with these 3 points:

1. Scripture is clear enough for the simplest person to live by. This doesn't mean that everyone understands its deepest points but everyone can understand the basic truths that God is communicating.

2. Scripture is deep enough for readers of the highest intellectual ability. There is much to ponder and try to comprehend.

3. Scripture is clear in essential matters. The Bible clearly teaches us things like — God is holy. Man is sinful. Jesus was God's Son. He was the sacrifice for our sins. The only way to the Father is through Him. Jesus is coming back! Heaven is real!

<u>The Bible alone is sufficient to equip a believer in living out the Christian life.</u> *The sufficiency of Scripture means that Scripture contains all the words of God He intended His people to have at each stage of redemptive history and that it now contains all the words of God we need for salvation, for trusting Him perfectly, and for obeying Him perfectly.[4]*

What did Jesus say about the sufficiency of Scripture in Matthew 4:4?

<u>The Bible is inerrant and infallible.</u> *The Bible is without error in its original manuscripts. When all the facts are fully known, the Bible will be seen to be true in every way. Article 11 of the Chicago Statement on Biblical Inerrancy (1978) says: "We affirm that Scripture, having been given by divine inspiration, is infallible, so that, far from misleading us, it is true and reliable in all the matters it addresses."[5]*

Why would the Bible be inerrant and infallible, based on 2 Peter 1:20-21?

<u>The Bible has been preserved through the centuries as the written record of God's special revelation for His people.</u> *This is the doctrine of preservation, which assures us that no inspired words of God have been lost in the past and await rediscovery.[6]*

What is guaranteed according to Isaiah 40:8?

This has been a brief look at several of the specific doctrines regarding the Holy Bible. I would encourage you to read more on Bibliology in John MacArthur's Biblical Doctrine, *or Wayne Grudem's* Systematic Theology.

What are we to do with the Word of God, and what does it do with us, according to 1 Thessalonians 2:13?

What should our attitude be as we read and hear the Word of God, based on Isaiah 66:2?

There are many more wonderful, exciting, and sobering truths about the Word of God in the Scriptures. And remember, the Word of God is living and active. So, even if you have read these truths before, they are still powerful today. We can, and must, keep reading our Bibles!

Here are a few more descriptions of and instructions from God's Word. Note what you learn.

Joshua 1:8

Proverbs 30:5-6

Jeremiah 23:29

2 Timothy 2:15

You are obviously studying the Bible, but what other ways are you engaging with God's Word?

How about singing God's Word? Make up your own tunes, or find some Scriptures set to music. You probably already know the tune for Psalm 119:105: "Thy word is a lamp unto my feet, And a light unto my path." NAS

Let's close our lesson today with an old hymn of thankfulness for the precious word of God. It summarizes much of what we've learned from Hebrews 4:12.

> Holy Bible, book divine, precious treasure, thou art mine;
> Mine to tell me whence I came; mine to teach me what I am.
>
> Mine to chide me when I rove; mine to show a Savior's love;
> Mine thou art to guide and guard; mine to punish or reward.
>
> Mine to comfort in distress; suffering in this wilderness;
> Mine to show, by living faith, man can triumph over death.
>
> Mine to tell of joys to come, and the rebel sinner's doom;
> O thou holy book divine, precious treasure, thou art mine.[7]

LESSON 13: AN INTRIGUING INTRODUCTION
HEBREWS 4:14-16

The sermon to the Hebrews is outstanding in its structure, logic, and substantiation of truth. If we were the Greek-speaking early Christians to whom this was written, it would be easier to recognize its excellence. But it's not a dissertation on the person of Jesus Christ.

It is a passionate explanation of who He is with the purpose of leading idle believers to a vibrant devotion to their Savior. Even if you are not struggling in your commitment to Jesus, this sermon warns you to stay focused on Him because of who He is and what He has done.

Believers over the centuries have appreciated the description found in Hebrews of Jesus who is the Great High Priest. Only here is His ministry explained to us with such detail and insight. It's the main topic of Hebrews 5:1-10:18.

In this lesson, we will look at the introduction that the pastor makes regarding the high priesthood of Jesus in Hebrews 4:14-16.

> It is important to remember that he does not intend these verses to be a full explanation. He wishes simply to impress his hearers with the magnitude of Christ's high priesthood and to intensify their interest in what is to come.[1]

Please pray that the Holy Spirit will give you a deeper understanding of Jesus as your High Priest.

Please read Hebrews 4:14-16. What details are we given about Jesus in verses 14 and 15?

His role:

His accomplishment:

His identity:

His compassion:

His humanity:

His perfection:

> Everything in this description is used to emphasize the immeasurable superiority of this High Priest. In the Greek Old Testament *great priest* is equivalent to *high priest*. Thus, there is redundancy in the expression "great high priest": [as if one is saying] "great great priest" or "high high priest." [2]

What details are we given about the throne in verse 16?

Its accessibility:

Its description:

Its offering:

There is so much in these verses! They paint a beautiful picture of what Jesus has done and where He is and what He does now. But, if we read them without an understanding of Jewish worship, we miss critical truths. We need to get some background from the Old Testament.

There was a special place in the tabernacle (and later in the temple) called the Holy of Holies. How was it separated from the other room in the tabernacle, and what was in it, according to Exodus 26:31-34?

Now we will look at the Lord's instructions for entering the Holy of Holies. You could read all of Leviticus 16, but I'll ask a few questions to highlight certain details.

What were the rules for the high priest regarding entering the Holy of Holies (also called the Most Holy Place), and why, according to Leviticus 16:2?

How was the high priest to enter the Holy of Holies and what was the purpose, according to the verses below?

Leviticus 16:3

Leviticus 16:6

Leviticus 16:16-17

Who could enter and how often could he enter the Holy of Holies, according to Leviticus 16:32-34?

> As the high priest passes through the holy place into the most holy place to stand before the divine presence on the Day of Atonement, Jesus has passed through the heavens to the divine presence. Unfortunately, "passed through the heavens" does not convey this idea in English.[3]

Now look at Hebrews 4:14-16 again, and describe in your own words what Jesus, the Great High Priest, has done, based on what you've learned about the actions of the high priest at the tabernacle.

High priests came and went. Over and over. Year after year. Offering sacrifices. To obtain mercy, grace, forgiveness for sins. The work of the high priest was never finished.

Until Jesus took on the work. Until Jesus became the Great High Priest. The one and only One who was without sin entered into the heavenly Holy of Holies on our behalf.

Hebrews 4:14-16 are a summarized introduction to the detailed discussion which we are about to encounter in the next five chapters. We will become intimately acquainted with the role of the high priest and the sacrifices he made, and we will gain an understanding of how Jesus is incomparably greater than any and all priests.

What are we to do as a result of Jesus' accomplishment as our Great High Priest?

    a. **Hebrews 4:14** _____

    b. **Hebrews 4:16** _____

    c. **Hebrews 4:16** _____

    d. **Hebrews 4:16** _____

What a beautiful, comforting encouragement. The throne room of the King of kings is open to us at all times. Jesus is there beside the God of all grace to welcome us, and He knows from His life on earth all the difficulties we experience. He will give us mercy and grace.

Please look up the definition for the following words:
Mercy: Strong's #1656
Greek word:
Greek definition:

Grace: Strong's #5485
Greek word:
Greek definition:

Does Hebrews 4:16 indicate that mercy and grace are one-time gifts to us, or are they ongoing? What does that mean about our need for them?

Based on all that we have studied in this lesson, how would you explain the mercy and grace that Jesus makes available to us? What is it? What makes it available to us? How do we receive it? When do we need it?

And now, please take time to take advantage of the amazing mercy and grace we are offered. Boldly enter the throne room of grace, bowing before your God and Savior, and make your requests known.

Thank you, Jesus.

LESSON 14: WHAT WE ALL NEED
HEBREWS 5:1-11

We are about to study and consider religious practices for Israelites which began roughly about 3500 years ago under Moses' supervision. And we will see how Jesus, who lived on earth about 2000 years ago, was appointed in a special way to carry out those ancient religious practices.

This sounds like ancient history. Is it relevant for us today? I think there is one all-important question that will reveal the critical need for understanding and applying the truths found in the Israelite's religion.

Is a person basically good or bad?

Begin thinking about your answer to that question. I'll come back to it soon.

Please pray that you will hear and heed the ancient truths of God and submit to the conviction of the Holy Spirit.

Please read Hebrews 5:1-4. What do we learn about the high priest of Israel? Record your answers below.

How does he become a high priest? (verses 1, 4)

What is his role? (verses 1, 3)

What is his weakness and need? (verses 2-3)

How does he empathize with others? (verse 2)

Moses' brother Aaron was the first high priest appointed by God. We read about some of his responsibilities in a previous lesson. The following passage describes his actions on the Day of Atonement.

HCSB Leviticus 16:21-24 Aaron will lay both his hands on the head of the live goat and confess over it all the Israelites' wrongdoings and rebellious acts—all their sins. He is to put them on the goat's head and send it away into the wilderness by the man appointed for the task. ²²The goat will carry on it all their wrongdoings into a desolate land, and he will release it there. ²³Then Aaron is to enter the tent of meeting, take off the linen garments he wore when he entered the most holy place, and leave them there. ²⁴He will bathe his body with water in a holy place and put on his clothes. Then he must go out and sacrifice his burnt offering and the people's burnt offering; he will make atonement for himself and for the people.

According to Leviticus 16:21-24:
How are sins described?

How did Aaron offer sacrifices for sins?

According to Leviticus 23:26-32, what instructions were given regarding the importance of the Day of Atonement?

Do you have any Jewish friends, neighbors, or coworkers who observe the Day of Atonement as a solemn day of repentance?

> Israel's most awesome holy day, known as Yom Kippur or "The Day of Atonement," is an ever present theme woven throughout the pages of Scripture. Three and one-half millennia after its divine institution, Yom Kippur still wields a powerful influence over the culture and worship of Israel. But of even greater import, Yom Kippur provides a necessary backdrop for understanding the scope of the Messiah's payment for sin and the security of God's people today.[1]

The question I asked at the beginning of our lesson is important to consider now. Is a person basically good or bad? While individuals around the world might answer this based on their own personal point of view, the answer must come from God's truth. Every person is born basically bad. Sinful. Wicked. Evil. It's horrible, bad news!

Remember how sins were described in Leviticus 16:21? As wrongdoings and rebellious acts? The first wrong, rebellious action was committed by Adam and Eve when they rejected God's instruction to them. If you need a reminder of their sin, read Genesis 3.

What do you learn about sin from the following verses?

Deuteronomy 24:16

1 Samuel 15:23-24

Psalm 32:3

Romans 5:12

Ephesians 2:1

James 4:17

Our study of the ancient religion of the Israelites is absolutely relevant today because we have the same problem they had: sin. Understanding Jesus' role as our Great High Priest is appropriate because we need a representative to stand before God on our behalf, just as the Israelites did.

It's time for wonderful good news! Because of our desperate situation and inability to help ourselves, God sent His Son Jesus to earth and also appointed Him as the greatest High Priest for all eternity.

Please read Hebrews 5:5-11. What do we learn about Jesus as High Priest for all people on earth? Record your answers below.

How did he become our High Priest? (verses 5, 6, 10)

What is His role? (verses 6, 8, 9, 10)

What was His weakness and need? (verses 7, 8)

How does He empathize with others? (verses 7, 8)

I hope you can see that the pastor writing his message to the Hebrews was comparing our superior High Priest to the hundreds of earthly high priests in the Israelites' religious practices.

> The Hebrew Christians who received this letter were sorely tempted to return to the religion of their fathers. After all, any Jew could travel to Jerusalem and see the temple and the priests ministering at the altar. Here was something real, visible, concrete.
>
> When a person is going through persecution, as these Hebrew Christians were, it is much easier to walk by sight than by faith. Some of us have doubted the Lord under much less provocation than these people were enduring.
>
> The central theme of Hebrews is the priesthood of Jesus Christ, what He is now doing in heaven on behalf of His people. Is the high priestly ministry of Christ superior to that of Aaron and his successors? Yes, it is.[2]

Please read the entire passage again: Hebrews 5:1-11.

What did the earthly high priests have to do that Jesus did not have to do?

How was the appointment of Jesus similar to that of the Israelite priests?

How was the appointment of Jesus different from that of the Israelite priests?

What was the difference in the sacrifice made by the Israelite priests (Hebrews 5:3) and the sacrifice made by Jesus (Hebrews 5:7)?

There are many remarkable characteristics of Jesus described in this passage, and it's still just a brief overview of His extraordinary accomplishment. The pastor has been laying the foundation of the superiority of Jesus as our Great High Priest and will continue to expound on this teaching and explain more about Melchizedek, after a brief rebuke to his readers.

Before we move on to his exhortation, let's summarize what we've learned so far about the High Priesthood of Jesus.

How is Jesus described in the following verses?

Hebrews 2:17-18

Hebrews 3:1-2

Hebrews 4:14-15

Summarize briefly how Jesus is described in Hebrews 5:1-11.

Please comment on the question I asked previously: Are people basically good or bad?

And consider the actions of Jesus as our High Priest. Why is it important to understand Jesus' role as High Priest?

How would you describe His actions for you personally?

One phrase in the passage we've been studying sums it all up: Jesus is the Source of Eternal Salvation. He alone gives salvation—rescuing us from sin and death. He alone is from heaven, sinless, and able to be the source—all that we need. He alone provides eternal—permanent—access into the throne room of our holy God. Why would you turn to any lesser priest or person or point of view?

WARNING – WARNING – WARNING

LESSON 15: ON TO MATURITY: THE THIRD WARNING
HEBREWS 5:11-6:12

In this year that I have been writing this workbook, the United States experienced the closing of a much-loved store—Toys R Us. Adults recalled being children who were thrilled to enter the giant toy land. Parents reminisced over the joy of seeing the delighted eyes of their children. I personally remembered the special date nights with my husband as we shopped for Christmas gifts for our children. Do you remember their jingle? "I don't wanna grow up, I'm a Toys R Us kid, they've got a million toys at Toys R Us that I can play with...."

That was good marketing! A catchy tune, identification with the store, and a wish that both children and adults express at times. But to say "I don't wanna grow up" is bad theology. It's the wrong attitude to have in our Christian lives.

So, the pastor to the Hebrews will tell his readers—stop acting like children! He'll urge them to act their age. Let's see if we need to apply his instruction to our own lives.

Please pray that you will hear and heed the word of God and the voice of the Holy Spirit.

The rebuke and exhortation from the pastor are found in Hebrews 5:11-6:12. This passage is one whole train of thought with 4 different sections. We will spend several lessons covering it.

Please read Hebrews 5:11-6:12.

What is the main problem pointed out by the pastor? He repeats it in Hebrews 5:11 and 6:12.

"You have become _____." Hebrews 5:11

"Do not become _____." Hebrews 6:12

Both of these verses use the exact same word in the Greek — nōthros.

Please look up the definition for the following word:
Nōthros: Strong's #3576
Greek word:
Greek definition:

> The adjective "dull" comes from two words: *ne* ("not") and *otheo* (to push). A dull person, therefore, has no push or drive; he is slow or sluggish. The readers were dull in the realm of hearing.... They were once alert to the voice of God, but their persistent doubts caused them to become restricted in their capacity to receive truth.[1]

The pastor rebukes his readers for being spiritually apathetic and lazy. This was stunting their spiritual growth. The pastor repeatedly emphasizes the need to pay attention to, trust, and obey the voice of God throughout his letter to the Hebrews. (Hebrews 2:1; 3:7-8, 15; 4:2, 7) They have been "hard of hearing" God's word to them.

It is very dangerous to be disinterested in God's Word. What might be some warning signs that you are becoming "hard of hearing" regarding the Bible and the voice of God?

On the other hand, what demonstrates your hunger for intimacy with and obedience to the Lord?

The pastor points out the spiritual immaturity resulting from their laziness in Hebrews 5:11-14.

Pastor Wiersbe uses the following phrases to describe the spiritual immaturity of the Hebrew readers.[2] Record the problems from the scriptures referenced.

Dullness toward the Word: Hebrews 5:11 –

Inability to Share: Hebrews 5:12a –

A "baby food" diet: Hebrews 5:12b-13 –

Unskillful in using the Word: Hebrews 5:14 –

The pastor to the Hebrews told them they were old enough to know better! They had been saved and had been learning God's truth long enough to be able to teach others. They already had a good foundation in the basic principles of the Christian faith.

Do you believe that "you ought to be teachers?" What does Matthew 28:18-20 tell you? How are you sharing the truths you have already learned?

The pastor wanted the Hebrews to skillfully apply the truth they already knew to their current situation. The more practice we have, the better we will become at using God's Word to direct and comfort us in our daily lives.

How do you use Scripture to guide you in decision-making and enduring trials? Can you give an example of how a specific verse was meaningful to you in a particular situation?

"I don't wanna grow up . . . ." Yes, I do! While there are things about childhood that are sweet and fun, there are even better things in store for those who grow up in the grace of God. The best is yet to come.

Please read Hebrews 6:1-4.

What is the goal the pastor urges the Hebrews toward? "Let us go on to _____."

I have been delighted to see that almost every commentary highlights an important truth in this exhortation. The Greek verb used is passive. And a better translation of the phrase above is "let us be carried forward."

Based on that information and Hebrews 6:4, who is doing the work in our lives to get us to the goal of perfection?

> The passive implies the agency of God and conveys the thought of surrender to God's active influence, rather than the personal striving for a goal. The term teleiotēs [perfection] describes a goal rather than a process. This is the accomplishment of God through Jesus Christ. [3]

I am so very thankful that my perfection is God's work. My role is cooperation and surrender.

What do the following verses tell us about God's goal for us?

Matthew 5:48

Philippians 1:6

So, we're moving forward! The Hebrews were told to press on and stop acting like lazy children.

According to Hebrews 6:1-2, what two actions did they have to take to cooperate with God's work in their lives?

*What does that mean? I've wondered about these phrases every time I've read them. But doing some research has helped me gain understanding. I think it would be so helpful if the English translations added one little word which commentators say give us the meaning of the first action to be taken. "Let us leave **standing** the elementary teaching about the Christ...."*

The pastor did not tell his readers to disregard what they had already learned. They were to build on that foundation. And what was the foundation? He listed six teachings that he will build on himself in the coming discussion of the priesthood of Jesus.

Let's get a preview.

Regarding repentance from dead works, what does the pastor tell us that Jesus our High Priest accomplished for us? See Hebrews 9:14.

Regarding faith in God, the pastor has much to say in Hebrews 11. But what does he tell us Jesus does regarding our faith? See Hebrews 12:2.

Regarding baptisms (which would be better translated as washings), what does the pastor teach in Hebrews 9:9-10 (the Israelite religious practices) and Hebrews 9:11, 14, 10:22 (Jesus' priesthood)?

Regarding the laying on of hands, the Mosaic law stipulated that a person should "put his hand upon the head of the burnt offering," namely the animal sacrifice (Leviticus 1:4). This was to transfer the sin to the animal and provide forgiveness. What does the pastor teach about Jesus' sacrifice? See Hebrews 10:17-19.

Regarding the resurrection of the dead and of eternal judgment, what does the pastor say that our High Priest Jesus has done and will do? See Hebrews 9:27-28.

When the readers of this sermon reviewed these six topics, they had the background and foundation upon which to build a better understanding of Jesus' superior priesthood. It has helped me to see that the pastor had a purpose for every word he communicated. Perhaps he was even stirring up their curiosity so that they would be eager to learn more about their great salvation.

I think the pastor shared Paul's perspective given in these references:

^{NLT} **1 Corinthians 13:11** When I was a child, I spoke and thought and reasoned as a child. But when I grew up, I put away childish things.

^{NLT} **Colossians 1:28** So we tell others about Christ, warning everyone and teaching everyone with all the wisdom God has given us. We want to present them to God, perfect in their relationship to Christ.

Please read the full exhortation from the pastor again in Hebrews 5:11-6:12.

You can see that we have more to examine in this important warning!

Please close this lesson with a prayer to apply what you have already learned.

LESSON 16: A Very Sober Warning
Hebrews 6:4-6

My dear friend, I love studying God's Word with you. It delights me to discover the deep, rich blessings that God has provided for us through His Son Jesus and His Holy Spirit. I enjoy praising Him for His goodness and grace. And, by the end of today's lesson, I anticipate doing that with you!

We have some hard work ahead of us though because the 3 verses we will examine are referred to as one of the most disputed passages in the New Testament. I have not rushed my behind-the-scenes study. I have been studying it, reading commentaries, contemplating, and praying about these verses during our study of the first five chapters of Hebrews. I will offer my interpretation to you humbly and give you the chance to make your own decision. I have read at least 7 different possible explanations of this warning. I think there are even more than that.

Especially today, please pray that the Holy Spirit will give you understanding of the Word of God and that you will heed His warning.

Repetition is a good teacher. Please read Hebrews 5:11-6:12. Remember that this is one train of thought including a rebuke and an exhortation. The problem was nōthros: disinterest in the word of God.

The first thing we need to do is get an overview of the one sentence found in Hebrews 6:4-6.

The first word in the Greek is adunaton – meaning impossible. As the first word in the sentence it is emphasized.

What is it impossible to do? See the action verbs in Hebrews 6:6.

    It is impossible to _____

How are the people in this sentence described? See Hebrews 6:4-5.

1. Those who were _____
2. Those who _____
3. Those who _____
4. Those who _____
5. Those who _____

What are the people in this sentence actively doing? See Hebrews 6:6.

1. They are _____

2. And they are _____

There are several different interpretations of the meaning of the phrases describing the people. The big question is whether they are true Christians or not.

*The pastor writing the Hebrews does not give us definitions, but he does use his Greek language carefully. The five descriptions above are from aorist plural participles which tell us that the pastor is referring to **other** people who have already experienced these things in their lives.*

How do we know that the pastor is **not** referring to his readers? See Hebrews 6:9.

That's good news. But it also means that he was offering this warning as a protection for them so that they would not suffer the consequences.

Was the pastor describing true Christians in Hebrews 6:4-5? Pastor Wiersbe has the most concise explanation of the participles used in these verses. Let's consider his comments and look at a few cross-references.

- They were "enlightened." The "once" means "enlightened once and for all." The way this same verb is used in Hebrews 10:32 indicates an experience of true salvation.[1]

What do you learn from Hebrews 10:32 and 2 Corinthians 4:6?

- They "tasted of the heavenly gift," and "tasted the good word of God, and the powers of the world [age] to come." To claim that these people "tasted but did not eat" is to base interpretation on one meaning of an English word. God permitted His Son to "taste death for every man." (Hebrews 2:9) Surely Jesus Christ did not simply sample death on the cross! "Taste" carries the idea of "experience." These Hebrew believers had experienced the gift of salvation, the Word of God, and the power of God. Doesn't this describe authentic salvation?[2]

What do you learn from John 6:53-54 and Ephesians 2:8-9?

81

- They "were made partakers of the Holy Ghost." To suggest that they only went along with the Holy Spirit to a certain extent is to ignore the simple meaning of the verb. It means "to become sharers."[3]

What did the pastor say his readers were partakers of in Hebrews 3:1 and 3:14?

The simple reading of the descriptions leads us to understand that the people described were true Christian believers. That's why this warning is so serious. That's also why it is controversial. Could the behavior and consequence actually happen to someone saved by grace?

The people described have "fallen away." This is translated in some versions as "apostasy" from aphistēmi but that is not the Greek word used in Hebrews 6:6. (See Lesson 10 for comments on apostasy.)

Parapesóntas from parapipto is the actual word used and means "to fall beside a person or thing; to slip aside; hence, to deviate from the right path, turn aside, wander."[4]

Some translations include the idea of "if" they have fallen away, but the participle parapesóntas is parallel to the others which attribute current characteristics to the people. There is no word in the Greek sentence indicating an "if" scenario.

The same Greek word, parapipto, is used in the Greek version of the Old Testament, the Septuagint, in a few verses in the book of Ezekiel.

What is the problem and the consequence in Ezekiel 15:8 where a form of the word parapipto is used?

Review the warning in Hebrews 6:4-6. What is the problem and the consequence?

What illustration is given in Hebrews 6:7-8 as an example of right and wrong behavior and the reward and punishment for them?

Well, we've looked at almost all the words in this warning. The devastating consequence for someone who has fallen away from faithfulness to the Lord is that "it is impossible to renew them to repentance." Does this mean that it is impossible for man to bring someone to repentance, but possible for God? If that were the case, then it wouldn't be much of a warning. And it is always God at work bringing someone to repentance anyway.

What does Romans 2:4 say?

Does Hebrews 6:6 refer to repentance for salvation? Or repentance for a particular sin?

What does the pastor tell us about repentance in Hebrews 12:16-17?

Esau sinned against the Lord by "despising his birthright" (Genesis 25:34). And when he regretted his action, it could not be undone. But Esau was not cut off from his relationship with the Lord, even though it was not what it could have been. The Lord gave Esau the hill country of Seir as his possession (Joshua 24:4), and Esau named his son Eliphaz, which could mean "God is fine gold" or "God is his strength."

Please consider these thoughts from Dr. Robert Gromacki:

> Concerning the fallen individuals (Heb. 6:5), the author dogmatically declared that it was "impossible . . . to renew them again to repentance." There is a repentance which is essential to salvation (Mark 1:15; Acts 2:38; 2 Pet. 3:9). There is also a repentance for a sinning Christian, fostered by a godly sorrow, which can restore him to divine blessing and fellowship (2 Cor. 7:9-10).
>
> A believer can lose the possibility of repentance through deliberate disobedience.
>
> Saul forfeited for himself and his posterity the possibility of kingly rule over Israel when he dared to officiate as a priest (1 Sam. 13:13-14). Esau lost any future opportunity of spiritual leadership when he sold his birthright to Jacob (Heb. 12:16-17). In fact, he "found no place of repentance, though he sought it carefully with tears" (Heb. 12:17). Israel could not go into Canaan once they refused to do so at Kadesh-Barnea.
>
> Even though people may change their minds after they recognize the consequences of their deeds, God forbids them from recovering their lost opportunities.[5]

Have you been thinking deeply about the warning given in Hebrews 6:4-6? I know that the pastor wanted the very best for his brothers and sisters in Christ. And he cared enough about their lives to give them a sober warning of what could happen if they didn't shake off their sluggishness.

We haven't finished with this controversial sentence. In the next lesson, we will consider various views of its meaning.

But let's end this lesson with a review of the incomparable greatness of the Source of our Eternal Salvation. We who are true believers can rejoice over the attributes and actions of our great Savior.

Please read Hebrews 1:1-2:1 and record your praise and thanksgiving for Him.

LESSON 17: A Lot to Think About
Hebrews 6:4-12

How can we make our study of the difficult verses in Hebrews 6:4-6 exciting and encouraging? Our attitude as we approach the holy word of God is very important. Haven't we been learning that the readers of Hebrews were "dull of hearing?" Lazy, apathetic, disinterested.

There are many things in life that are challenging and hard work, but worth the effort. Exercise! Child-rearing! Even some simple things like gardening and house-cleaning are in that category for me.

I hope to help you think through the different views of the interpretation of Hebrews 6:4-6 with an attitude of discovery. Let's search for rich treasures in God's Word! It will be worth the effort.

Please pray to hear and heed the word of the Lord and the voice of the Holy Spirit as He leads you into further understanding of His truth.

I wonder what your favorite verse is about salvation? Because the verses we're studying are so intertwined with God's saving work in our lives, we will look at many beautiful statements about salvation in this lesson. I'll ask you about your favorite verse again later.

I've created a chart on the next page with the different views of Hebrews 6:4-6. As we consider the options, we should keep a few important hermeneutical (interpretational) questions in mind.

1. ***Question:*** *What is the genre or type of writing here?*

    Answer: *At this point in his sermon, the pastor is exhorting and warning his readers. We should consider the **purpose** of the view in the chart.*

2. ***Question:*** *What is the context of this passage?*

    Answer: *It's the exhortation as mentioned above, and also the whole book of Hebrews with its many references to the Old Testament.*

3. ***Question:*** *What do other passages teach about this topic?*

    Answer: *We'll look at cross-references.*

Option	Description	Concern with this view
True believer loses salvation *Purpose of this view? Warns readers not to fall away because of irrevocable loss of eternal salvation	v.4-5 describe actual experiences of salvation, falling away means deliberate choice to reject Jesus' saving work	Major teaching in Hebrews is that of the finished work of Jesus as High Priest, source of eternal salvation
Professing Believer (Unbeliever) rejects confession about Christ *Purpose of this view? Warns any readers who are not true believers that falling away would cause irrevocable loss of salvation, prompts decision for real faith and salvation	v.4-5 describe experiences of those associated with community of true believers, but those who fall away have not experienced true salvation	If this describes unbelievers, they are already without salvation, so how can they lose it? "The opportunity to repent for salvation is open to the unsaved right up to the point of their physical death."[1]
Only applies to 1st Century Jews *Purpose of this view? Warns them to accept Christ as their Savior	v.4-6 address Jews associated with the true believing Christian community, these Jews have not made a commitment to faith in Christ	There are many references to the readers as holy brothers. If this describes unbelieving Jews, they are already without salvation, so how can they lose it?
True believer who falls away, can repent *Purpose of this view? Warning readers that falling away will jeopardize their fellowship with God.	v.4-5 describe actual experiences of salvation and falling away. Repentance is impossible while they are actively putting Christ to shame. "The writer did not say that these people could never be brought to repentance. He said that they could not be brought to repentance while they were treating Jesus Christ in such a shameful way."[2]	This minimizes the warning, and is no different from any unconfessed sin that hinders a believer's fellowship with God.
Hypothetical situation *Purpose of this view? Shocking warning to prompt readers to be diligent in their faith	v.4-6 describe something that cannot actually happen	There are other severe warnings in Hebrews which are not hypothetical and include the discipline of God. If this is not describing something that can really happen, it is not really a warning at all.
True Believer Under Discipline *Purpose of this view? Warns readers of grave danger of falling away and experiencing severe discipline from God	v.4-5 describe actual experiences of salvation, v.6 describes sin of falling away which brings reproach upon Christ, it is impossible to restore believer to previous state before his sin	If repentance in v.6 refers to repentance for salvation, then this view would be inaccurate.

Verses to Consider:	Note truths about salvation
Ephesians 1:4-5; 13-14 2 Thessalonians 2:13-14 Romans 8:28-39 John 10:28-30 1 John 2:25	
2 Peter 3:9 1 Timothy 2:4 Acts 4:12	
Romans 10:11-13	
1 John 1:9 James 5:16	
Hebrews 2:2-3 Hebrews 10:26-30	
1 Corinthians 11:30-32 Hebrew 12:5-6 Hebrews 12: 25	

Almost every verse you looked at in the chart contains a beautiful treasure in regards to our salvation.

What verse(s) stand out to you as your favorite? You can add to the list above if you'd like.

The pastor writing to his dear friends was seriously concerned about their spiritual lives and their faithfulness to our faithful Savior. The book of Hebrews fixes our eyes on Jesus so that we will hold fast to Him and Him alone. He has provided us with so great a salvation.

Let's bring our examination of Hebrews 6:4-6 to a close. I'll share my conclusions with you, in case you haven't figured out my view yet.

But first, what is your conclusion? And why? You can choose from the chart above or explain your understanding. You probably won't be alone in your choice. I have a list of about 20 commentators' views who have overlapping and also varying perspectives.

Here's the conclusion that I've come to: True believers can commit sin by falling away from the Lord and then come under His severe discipline in which their lives on earth will lack the blessing they could have had through obedience to Him. But true believers will not lose their salvation. This is the last view mentioned in the chart above, and a perspective shared by Dr. Robert Gromacki and J. Dwight Pentecost.

As I contemplated the whole context of the warning, the serious concern expressed in Hebrews 3:12-13 and the teaching regarding the discipline of the Lord in Hebrews 12:6-25 influenced my thoughts. And the Israelites who rebelled against the Lord at Kadesh Barnea were the people of God who were given as the example of what not to do.

The Israelites fell away from faithfulness to the Lord through unbelief, leading to disobedience and the Lord did not allow them to enter the Promised Land. That generation died in the wilderness as discipline from the Lord. Even Moses, because of his sin of unbelief was denied entry into the Promised Land (Numbers 20:11-12).

In addition to the example of the Israelites impacting my view, there are many verses guaranteeing eternal life. They promise eternal life because of God's work through Jesus Christ and His Holy Spirit; this gives me assurance that one who has been brought from death to life by the Spirit of God cannot lose that life.

Hallelujah!

I also think that the warning is such that it persuades believers to take it personally and make appropriate changes in their behavior.

What do you think is the most sobering, challenging, and motivating view of Hebrews 6:4-6 for a true believer?

I came to the conclusion that the most extreme warning to me as a believer would be that God would severely discipline me if I sin treacherously against Him through rebellion and apathy.

What motivates you to be actively engaged in faithful obedience to God's Word?

Is there any change you need to make in your attitude towards the word of God, the work of Christ, or your response to the Holy Spirit?

Let's pay attention to what the Lord says to us!

How is the good result of obedience illustrated in Hebrews 6:7?

Please read Hebrews 5:11-6:12 once more.

How would you (briefly) summarize the main point the pastor is making to his readers?

*It seems like a long time ago that I mentioned that this portion of Hebrews consists of four sections. We've looked at three of them now. We've seen the **alert** (that they were dull of hearing, Hebrews 5:11-14), the **prompt** (to press on to perfection, Hebrews 6:1-3), the **warning** (not to fall away, Hebrews 6:4-8), and now we'll see **assurance** of God's faithfulness in Hebrews 6:9-12.*

How does the pastor motivate the believers toward the goal of perfection in Hebrews 6:9, and how does this remind them of God's work in their lives?

When you are reprimanded for something, do you respond with "but what about when I did that other thing right?" What did the pastor tell his readers that God was very aware of, according to Hebrews 6:10?

Can you see that the emphasis here is on the righteous, just nature of God to honor what is done for His name's sake? God is good and right in what He does.

In Hebrews 6:11-12, what is the believer's responsibility?

These truly are words of hope directing us to continue on for the treasure God has promised us. Keep going. Keep working hard! Exercise instructors remind their classes throughout the workout to work hard, don't stop, press on, smile . . . just keep moving all the way to the end!

We will inherit the promises of God through faith and patience.

With the mention of the word promises, the pastor is ready to expound upon God's oath to Abraham, which will lead his comments directly back to the topic of the High Priesthood of Jesus.

Before we leave the encouraging words of Hebrews 6:11-12, please write them as a prayer for yourself to continue on toward God's goal for your future.

LESSON 18: TRUST THE PROMISES OF GOD
HEBREWS 6:13-20

How often has someone said "you can trust me" to encourage you that they are reliable and you are safe with them? Or perhaps friends and family have guaranteed their commitment to you with "I promise." I hope that these people have kept their word and not let you down. But people do disappoint sometimes.

We will see our pastor encourage his readers to press on to perfection by showing them that our faithful God keeps His promises. What magnificent promises they are!

Let us be encouraged by this Scripture that God is 100% reliable and we are eternally safe with Him.

Please pray that you will not be dull of hearing the word of God and that you will depend on the enlightenment of the Holy Spirit.

Please read Hebrews 6:12-7:1 below. I have included the verses before and after the passage we are studying so that you will see the connections and transitions in the pastor's sermon. **Highlight** all forms of the words **promise, swear,** and **oath.** (Use one color, not three.)

^NIV **Hebrews 6:12 - 7:1** We do not want you to become lazy, but to imitate those who through faith and patience inherit what has been promised. ¹³When God made his promise to Abraham, since there was no one greater for him to swear by, he swore by himself, ¹⁴saying, "I will surely bless you and give you many descendants." ¹⁵And so after waiting patiently, Abraham received what was promised. ¹⁶Men swear by someone greater than themselves, and the oath confirms what is said and puts an end to all argument. ¹⁷Because God wanted to make the unchanging nature of his purpose very clear to the heirs of what was promised, he confirmed it with an oath. ¹⁸God did this so that, by two unchangeable things in which it is impossible for God to lie, we who have fled to take hold of the hope offered to us may be greatly encouraged. ¹⁹We have this hope as an anchor for the soul, firm and secure. It enters the inner sanctuary behind the curtain, ²⁰where Jesus, who went before us, has entered on our behalf. He has become a high priest forever, in the order of Melchizedek. ⁷:¹This Melchizedek was king of Salem and priest of God Most High. He met Abraham returning from the defeat of the kings and blessed him.

The example of Abraham trusting God to keep His promise was important for several reasons. Abraham is the father of the Israelite nation, the Hebrews. Jews trace their lineage back to him. And Abraham, even with his faults and big mistakes, is honored by God as one who had faith in Him despite adverse circumstances.

What was God's promise to Abraham in Genesis 12:1-4, and Abraham's response?

What was the problem for Abraham, the promise of God, and the response of Abraham according to Genesis 15:1-6?

In Romans 4:18-25, how did Paul describe the faith of Abraham and the reason he is an example to us?

Based on Hebrews 6:11-15, and the passages from Genesis and Romans above, how is Abraham a powerful example to the readers to "show diligence for the final realization of their hope?"

Do you know the children's Sunday School song about Father Abraham? Because God kept His promises to Abraham, he had many sons! And because Jesus was a descendant of Abraham, our trust in His salvation makes us a son of Abraham by faith and adoption into the family of God (Romans 4:16). So let's all praise the Lord—with all our heart, soul, mind, strength, and body!

> Father Abraham had many sons, Many sons had Father Abraham
> I am one of them and so are you, So let's all praise the Lord!
> Right arm, left arm, right foot, left foot, chin up, turn around, sit down! [1]

We have much to praise the Lord for! And we will see even more as we look at the passage in Hebrews 6:12-7:1 again.

Please read Hebrews 6:12-7:1 on the previous page, and **highlight** (with one color), the **name of God** and phrases that describe **His attributes and actions.**

What is the pastor emphasizing about God in these verses?

> He alone shall make any affirmation regarding Himself, since He alone has unerringly exact knowledge of His own nature. God alone therefore is the strongest security first for Himself, and in the next place for His deeds also, so that He naturally swore by Himself when giving assurance regarding Himself, a thing impossible for anyone else.[2]

The pastor gives his readers and us a great boost of encouragement in our faith by drawing attention to the character of God. What are the "two unchangeable things" about Him referred to in Hebrews 6:18? I always have trouble with this because I can only count one thing!

Studying in community with other believers is so helpful, even when they speak through their books. F. F. Bruce (1910-1990), Professor of Biblical Criticism and Exegesis at the University of Manchester, England says:

> The "two unchangeable things" from which this encouragement is derived are (a) the promise of God (for "it is impossible for God to lie"), and (b) the oath by which His promise is confirmed.[3]

Do you understand? We can trust the promises of God because first of all, God said it Himself and He doesn't lie when He makes a promise. And secondly, He guaranteed that He would keep His promise by swearing an oath upon Himself. He promised that He would keep His promise!

What is the result of this promised promise of God? What do we have according to Hebrews 6:18-20?

The world is a sinking ship! We need to hold on to something that won't let us drown in its sin and despair and suffering. Our lifeline is hope, attached to an anchor. The pastor uses this illustration to paint the picture of what Jesus does and where He is.

According to Hebrews 6:18-20:

What is our need?

What is our help?

How is the anchor described?

Where is the anchor?

> "We are moored to an immoveable object"—and that immoveable object is the throne of God Himself, established in the heavenly holy of holies, the counterpart in the eternal order to the inner sanctuary of the wilderness tabernacle, shut off from the outer sanctuary by the heavy curtain behind which dwelt the invisible presence of the God of Israel. And our hope is fixed there because Jesus is there, seated, as we have already been told, at "the right hand of the Majesty on high" (1:3).[4]

Let's meditate on the truth of Hebrews 6:18-20. Please illustrate this verse in some way. Draw a picture or write the verse out with images and special lettering. Use colors! Or if you like music or poetry, you could compose a few lyrics expressing its truth. Take time to reflect on this trustworthy promise of God.

Let us hold fast to the hope set before us. What is our hope? What is the promise of God that He has promised? There are hundreds of beautiful, comforting, amazing promises of God throughout the Bible. Do your own study on the promises of God sometime! I did it during the month of December a few years ago. They truly will strengthen your faith and hope.

But there is one particular promise that the pastor is emphasizing as extremely important for his readers to understand and hold fast.

What is God's unalterable promise according to Psalm 110:4, Hebrews 5:10, and Hebrews 6:20?

And with that reminder of who the pastor has much to say about, we will close this lesson. I hope you are eager to learn about the importance of Jesus our High Priest according to the order of Melchizedek!

LESSON 19: MYSTERIOUS MELCHIZEDEK
HEBREWS 7:1-24

You have been prepared! The pastor said he had much to say about Melchizedek and he wasn't exaggerating! We have come to the main exposition of the sermon to the Hebrews. Describing the priesthood of Melchizedek sets the stage for the in-depth explanation of Jesus' priestly work.

Ancestry.com is doing big business these days as people are very interested in discovering their roots. They say they "combine DNA results and the largest collection of records for the best insight into your genealogy and origins."[1] Where did you come from? What's your family's story? Inquiring minds want to know.

There wouldn't be much information on Melchizedek available on Ancestry.com! What does the Bible tell us about him?

Please pray that the Holy Spirit will give you a deeper understanding of God's Word and of Jesus as your High Priest.

Please read Hebrews 7:1-4.

What are the specific details given about Melchizedek? Fill in the blanks below:

His roles: _____ of Salem and _____ of the Most High God

    met _____ and _____ him

    received _____ from Abraham

Meaning of his names: king of _____

        and king of Salem _____

His ancestry: no _____, no _____, no _____

Record of his birth and death: _____

His likeness to the Son of God is that he remains _____

He was a great man because even Abraham _____

The details above were gleaned by the author of Hebrews from Genesis 14:14-20 and Psalm 110:4. Please read Genesis 14:14-20. How would you explain who Melchizedek was based on Genesis and Hebrews?

There are two concepts that it will be helpful to define and then determine which one applies to Melchizedek.

Theophany – *a visible appearance or manifestation of God, particularly in the Old Testament. Also called a Christophany when there is a visible appearance of Pre-incarnate Jesus.*[2]

Typology – *an actual historical event or person that in some ways symbolizes or anticipates a later occurrence; particularly, an Old Testament foreshadowing of a New Testament event.*[3]

Was there anything in Genesis 14:14-20 that indicated that Abraham saw a visible manifestation of God? Remember from our readings of Genesis 12:1-4 and 15:1-6 in a previous lesson that Abraham had heard the voice of God and obeyed His call. Which would you apply to Melchizedek, theophany or typology?

Are you satisfied with your answer? That probably depends on how your mind works and what you have heard about Melchizedek over the years. Please keep in mind that the book of Hebrews is about our High Priest Jesus Christ and nothing should distract us from our focus on His superiority over everyone.

> Our author's point is that so far as the record is concerned, Melchizedek typifies Christ [typology] because Genesis presents him as a functioning priest with no indication of beginning or ending or any dependence upon human pedigree. Thus, he is a remarkable picture of Christ and His priesthood, and for this reason God Himself made this connection in Psalm 110:4: "Thou art a priest forever according to the order of Melchizedek." [4]

Please put what we've looked at this far in your own words. How would you describe "the order of Melchizedek" and what this tells us about Jesus as High Priest?

But wait. There's more. Melchizedek was a priest of the Most High God during the lifetime of Abraham. About 400 years later, after Abraham, Isaac, Jacob and his sons died, Moses and Aaron led the Israelites out of Egypt. Moses and Aaron traced their genealogy back to Levi, son of Jacob, son of Isaac, son of Abraham.

What did the Lord do for the tribe of Levi, according to Deuteronomy 10:8-9 and 18:1-2?

According to Hebrews 7:5-7:

Whose genealogy is not traced back to Levi and Abraham?

Who blessed whom?

Who is superior?

Okay. Hang in there. I know it's hard to listen to someone else's ancestral heritage. Follow the lines and the logic though. When we get the details straight in our heads, they will impact our hearts.

Please read Hebrews 7:4-10.

Here are a few explanations about Hebrews 7:8-10.

^{NAS} **Hebrews 7:8** And in this case mortal men receive tithes – *Levitical priests are mortal: they continually die and are replaced.*

^{NAS} **Hebrews 7:8** But in that case one receives them, of whom it is witnessed that he lives on. – *We never read of Melchizedek other than as a living man, and Psalm 110:4 characterizes his priesthood as "forever." This characterizes the priesthood of Melchizedek as one that continues, rather than the temporary priesthood of each Levite who died.*

^{NKJ} **Hebrews 7:9-10** Even Levi, who receives tithes, paid tithes through Abraham, so to speak, ^{10}for he was still in the loins of his father when Melchizedek met him. – *The priesthood of Melchizedek is greater than the Levitical priesthood because Melchizedek received tithes from and blessed Levi centuries before he was born.*

What important aspect of the High Priesthood of Jesus stands out from the notes above?

According to Hebrews 7:11-12:

What did people receive under the Levitical priesthood?

Did the Levitical priesthood provide perfection?

What two changes did God set in motion with His oath in Psalm 110:4?

The Levitical priesthood could not bring about perfection in its priests or the people it served. So God made changes that would provide the perfection that all people need. I like the way the Complete Jewish Bible translates the idea of perfection; it refers to it as the goal to be reached. What perfection, what goal, does God desire for us? That we be perfect even as He is perfect (Matthew 5:48). In other words, to be like Him, pure, holy, free from sin. God brings this about through the sacrifice offered by the Great High Priest Jesus.

Still speaking of the change in the priesthood, who is being referred to and what points does the pastor make in Hebrews 7:13-14?

According to Hebrews 7:15-17, Jesus became a priest not on the basis of His ancestry, but on the basis of what?

What is the repeated detail in Hebrews 7:3, 8, and 16?

Look ahead just a little to Hebrews 7:25. What does the One who always lives do for us?

That's why the details of Jesus' priesthood are so important! He stands before our God on our behalf. Our salvation and our daily needs are in His hands. We'll look at this verse again later.

According to Hebrews 7:18-19:

What happened to the former commandment about the priesthood and why?

What has the change of the priesthood brought us?

There is a new system! It was promised by God, who promises to keep His promises—remember?

In the passage on the next page, **highlight** the **promise of God** in one color, and the **impact of that promise** in another color.

^HCSB^ **Hebrews 7:20-24** None of this happened without an oath. For others became priests without an oath, ²¹but He with an oath made by the One who said to Him: "The Lord has sworn, and He will not change His mind, 'You are a priest forever according to the order of Melchizedek.'" ²²So Jesus has also become the guarantee of a better covenant. ²³Now many have become Levitical priests, since they are prevented by death from remaining in office. ²⁴But because He remains forever, He holds His priesthood permanently.

There is nothing more certain and secure than the promise of God.

Out with the old, in with the new. A better covenant, a better hope.

The promise of God, rather than the lineage of man, makes Jesus the Superior High Priest.

Jesus lives and doesn't die. So He helps people forever!

LESSON 20: OUR PERSONAL PERFECT HIGH PRIEST
HEBREWS 7:25-29

In the midst of a lengthy, logical explanation of why Jesus is the superior High Priest, more excellent than the mere mortal Levitical priests, the pastor gives us an opportunity to recognize how meaningful this is to us.

All that Jesus is, all that His priesthood accomplishes, is personally applicable to our lives.

Please pray that you will trust the Holy Spirit to give you understanding of these precious and personal truths.

Please read Hebrews 7:24-29.

Jesus saves! To the uttermost! Completely! Forever! This is full, guaranteed, eternal salvation!

Please look up the meaning of the following word:
Save: Strong's #4982
Greek word:
Greek definition:

Why is Jesus able to save us forever and who does He save, according to Hebrews 7:24-25?

Who do you want Jesus to save? Make your requests known to Him now.

Jesus intercedes for us before the Lord. The word "intercede" means: to go to or meet a person, especially for the purpose of conversation, consultation, or supplication.[1] Can you picture it? Jesus represents you and me at the throne of God. He stands in front of God in my place. He died in my place on the cross so that I wouldn't have to bear the wrath of God. Now He stands in my place before God, speaking to God on my behalf. Conversing, consulting, and supplicating. Making requests for you and me.

Why can Jesus stand before the throne of God, according to Hebrews 7:26-27?

Remember that the pastor has already emphasized that Jesus is where He is now because He finished His work for us on earth.

Note Jesus' present location and place of His priestly ministry according to the verses below.

Hebrews 1:13

Hebrews 4:14

The apostle Paul understood the priestly ministry of Jesus as well. What encouragement did he give in Romans 8:31-35?

How did Jesus intercede for His disciples and us while He was on earth? Note His requests found in the passages below.

Luke 22:32

John 17:11-26

Jesus prayed for help for us because of our weaknesses. Because we struggle under temptation. Because we face trials and need perseverance. Because we need protection. Because we need sanctification and hope.

Do you have any specific prayer requests for Jesus to make on your behalf right now? Offer them to Him with thankfulness for His compassion for you.

Please don't miss the reason that Jesus can stand before God as our High Priest.

According to Hebrews 7:27-28:

What is the difference between Jesus and any other priest?

What did Jesus do that no other priest could do?

What is Jesus' all-important characteristic?

Because the pastor was writing to encourage his friends to persevere through difficult circumstances, he explained that Jesus had faced suffering and could be compassionate towards their trials. We've looked at these verses previously, but let's remember them as we are focusing on the ministry of our great High Priest.

What did Jesus experience and what is His description, according to the following verses?

Hebrews 2:9-10

Hebrews 2:17-18

Hebrews 4:14-15

Hebrews 5:7-10

I entitled this lesson: Our Personal, Perfect High Priest. I hope that you are beginning to grasp how intimately acquainted our Savior is with us and our needs. There has been no Levitical High Priest since AD 70 when the temple in Jerusalem was destroyed by the Romans. No priest of any religion can do what Jesus does. There is no one like Jesus.

The next verse in Hebrews is an incredible, exciting declaration of praise. I'd like to imagine that the pastor capitalized it, underlined it, and ended it with an exclamation point! I don't think they did those things when writing ancient Greek letters. But I can . . . .

^{NKJ} HEBREWS 8:1
<u>NOW THIS IS THE MAIN POINT OF THE THINGS WE ARE SAYING:</u>
<u>WE HAVE SUCH A HIGH PRIEST,</u>
<u>WHO IS SEATED AT THE RIGHT HAND</u>
<u>OF THE THRONE OF THE MAJESTY IN THE HEAVENS!</u>

Celebrate! We have a living, compassionate, perfect, personal High Priest! He knows us and cares for us and prays for us.

Please read Hebrews 7:1-8:1. Then write your response of praise to your personal, superior High Priest Jesus, who offered His life as the once and final sacrifice for your salvation. Please let the details with which we've filled our minds lead to devotion from our hearts.

LESSON 21: THE SANCTUARY, SACRIFICES, AND COVENANTS
HEBREWS 8:1-13

I hope you ended the last lesson on a high note of praise! There are usually songs and hymns that come to mind as I'm studying. Two of my systematic theology books include hymns which correlate to every topic. I love that. But I can't listen to music that has words as I am studying. It's too distracting! Sometimes I search for certain types of instrumental music to listen to online. I've been introduced to much new music that way.

One of the commentators who is "helping" me has described the next 3 chapters of Hebrews with the illustration of a symphony. It's so lovely that I will share his thoughts with you to help us with the next big section of teaching from the pastor.

Please pray that you will not be dull of hearing the word of God and that you will depend on the enlightenment of the Holy Spirit.

G. L. Cockerill says: "A careful preview will assist the contemporary reader in negotiating this richly rewarding section." [1] He's referring to Hebrews 8:1-10:18. It's not a quick easy read.

> The artistry of the pastor's presentation is like a symphony in three movements developing these three themes—sanctuary, sacrifice, and covenant. Each movement begins with the theme of sanctuary and ends with covenant. At the center of each is the ever-expanding theme of sacrifice. [2]
>
> When the author as conductor has finished his symphony, he would leave his hearers overwhelmed with the magnitude and wonder of this High Priest and ready at all cost to persevere through the benefits He affords. The pastor makes this purpose clear in the encore that follows (especially 10:19-25).[3]

Let's engage in a brief preview! In the outline on the next page, I have given you a few verses out of each movement. Perhaps you can imagine the sound of trumpets welcoming you into the sanctuary, the sound of violins signifying the sacrifice, and the sound of cymbals announcing the covenant.

Please read the verses and note what you learn regarding the topic given.

The Symphony of the Sanctuary, Sacrifice, and Covenant
1st Movement: Hebrews 8:1-13

    The Sanctuary – Hebrews 8:2

    Sacrifice – Hebrews 8:3

    Covenant – Hebrews 8:7-8

2nd Movement: Hebrews 9:1-22

    The Sanctuary – Hebrews 9:8-9

    Sacrifice – Hebrews 9:12

    Covenant – Hebrews 9:19-20

3rd Movement: Hebrews 9:23-10:18

    The Sanctuary – Hebrews 9:23-24

    Sacrifice – Hebrews 10:11-12

    Covenant – Hebrews 10:16-17

I'm so happy to have an outline to follow for the next few chapters. They are rich in their teaching about the most excellent work that Jesus our Great High Priest has accomplished. It is challenging, however, to absorb the truths because there is so much material, and so much is dependent on our understanding of the Old Testament.

We will press on though and learn what God permits us to learn! Little by little. Layer upon layer. One thing at a time! First, the pastor tells us about the sanctuary (called tabernacle in some translations). He mentions an earthly sanctuary and a heavenly sanctuary.

According to Hebrews 8:1-5:

How is the **heavenly** sanctuary described?

How is the **earthly** sanctuary described? How was it built?

What does Exodus 25:3-9 tell you that the **earthly** sanctuary was made with? And what was its purpose?

Does it sound like it would have been a very special sacred place?

Why is it hard to let go of something that has been meaningful to you, even when you recognize that there is something better in store?

Let's take a look at the biblical descriptions of the **heavenly** sanctuary. Note what you learn from the following verses:

Exodus 24:9-11

Isaiah 6:1-4

Daniel 7:9-10

Revelation 11:19

Which sanctuary is better, the earthly or the heavenly one?

If the earthly sanctuary required special sacrifices, what type of sacrifices would the heavenly sanctuary require?

I hope those questions help you see one aspect of the teaching from the pastor to the Hebrews. Jesus is the far superior High Priest, serving at the incomparably better heavenly sanctuary. No mere man was sufficient for that role.

Highlight the three phrases below describing the superiority of Jesus' priesthood.

^{NKJ} **Hebrews 8:6** But now He has obtained a more excellent ministry, inasmuch as He is also Mediator of a better covenant, which was established on better promises.

The good promise from God to Moses and the Israelites was that He would dwell among them and be their God (Exodus 25:8). That's amazing. And personal.

But God made an even better promise, which fulfills and supersedes His first promise. We refer to it as the new covenant, because that's what God calls it too!

Please read about the better promise, the new covenant, in Hebrews 8:7-13. The pastor quotes directly from Jeremiah 31:31-34.

According to Hebrews 8:7-13:

Summarize the problem with the first (old) covenant. (Hint: It really wasn't a problem with the covenant, but with the people.)

What aspect of the new covenant is similar to the old covenant?

Describe the better promises of the new covenant.

What does the pastor want his readers to recognize about the permanency of the old covenant?

There are a few things we need to make sure we understand about the Old Covenant before we reflect on the joys of the New Covenant.

Fill in the blanks next to the statements with one word which describes the Old Covenant, based on the information given.

_____ The "Old Covenant" was the Mosaic Law which included regulations for daily life as well as the rules of the Levitical priesthood and sacrifices. (Exodus 20-24, Leviticus)

_____ Everything given by God (including the laws, regulations, and promises of the Old Covenant) is good.

^{NAS}**James 1:17** Every good thing bestowed and every perfect gift is from above, coming down from the Father of lights, with whom there is no variation, or shifting shadow.

_____The Old Covenant had two important purposes. It instructed God's people to live according to His righteous standard and it revealed the nature of God, man, and the relationship between the two.[4]

How does Galatians 3:21-25 explain that the Old Covenant was a tutor, and never was intended to produce justification (righteousness) within the Israelite?

_____The Old Covenant was inadequate to change the human heart because it depended on man for its fulfillment.

How did the Israelites respond to the requirements of the covenant, according to Exodus 24:3?

What was the good intention of the Old Covenant (the law) according to Romans 8:3-4?

What was the problem with the Old Covenant (the law) according to Romans 8:3-4?

When Hebrews 8:13 says that the old is becoming obsolete, to what exactly is that referring? When did the Old Covenant become old? How does Hebrews 8:13 answer this question?

The Lord Himself changed the status of the Mosaic Covenant when He announced through Jeremiah that He would make a new covenant. Sometime around 600 BC, when Jeremiah gave the Lord's prophecy of the New Covenant, the Old Covenant started becoming obsolete. It had always been a temporary means of directing people to righteousness.

> These two covenants are not intended to coexist, but the second replaces the first. The verb translated "made . . . obsolete" connotes becoming old in the sense of losing its usefulness. Thus, here in Hebrews 8:13, the writer speaks of the old covenant as having gotten beyond its time of usefulness.[5]

The pastor wants his Christian brothers and sisters to recognize that the old way has been replaced, even superseded, by a new and better way through Jesus. And the old way, the Old Covenant, would soon "vanish away" when the Temple in Jerusalem was destroyed.

> If in fact the Jerusalem temple was still standing [at the time of writing Hebrews], if the priests of Aaron's line were still discharging their sacrificial duties there, then our author's words would be all the more telling. Jesus, and shortly after him Stephen, had foretold the downfall of the temple.[6]

Please make sure that you don't consider the words "old" and "obsolete" to mean that the Old Covenant is just junk. And let's be especially careful not to let the change in the covenants lead us to anti-Semitism. Jesus and His first followers, and so many afterward were all Jews.

How is the Old Covenant meaningful to you? What aspects are you thankful for? (Consider the Mosaic law, Ten Commandments, rules for worship, the Sabbath, yearly festivals.)

The first movement of the Symphony of the Sanctuary, Sacrifice, and Covenant has ended.

Are you ready to move into a discussion of the New Covenant? I am! The pastor, however, has much more to say about the Old Covenant. This will be good for us! The better we understand the procedures of the Old Covenant, the better we will understand Jesus' work as our High Priest.

And we will rejoice all the more in the New Covenant!

LESSON 22: THE IMPORTANCE OF THE OLD WAY
HEBREWS 9:1-10

Would you like to travel back in time and observe some of the old days and ways? I'd like to visit some moments in history but I wouldn't want to live in them.

In Hebrews 9:1-22, the pastor will describe the sacred, intricate and intimate practices of the Levitical high priests. The setting is the wilderness before the Israelites entered the Promised Land. Moses had received instructions for building the tabernacle and worshipping the Lord there.

Please pray that the Holy Spirit will give you understanding of truth and you will rejoice in your salvation.

We will look at the second movement of the symphony now and focus our attention on the sanctuary. Perhaps you can imagine the sounds of the shofar calling people to worship and drums beating as the sacrifice is presented. Then tambourines would celebrate the covenant!

2nd Movement: Hebrews 9:1-22
The Sanctuary – Hebrews 9:1-10
Sacrifice – Hebrews 9:11-15
Covenant – Hebrews 9:16-22

Please read Hebrews 9:1-10.

This is a description of a place of holiness and divine worship. The image below depicts the tabernacle in the wilderness. Label the rooms and furnishings as described in Hebrews 9:2-5.

A.

B.

C.

D.

E.

F.

G.

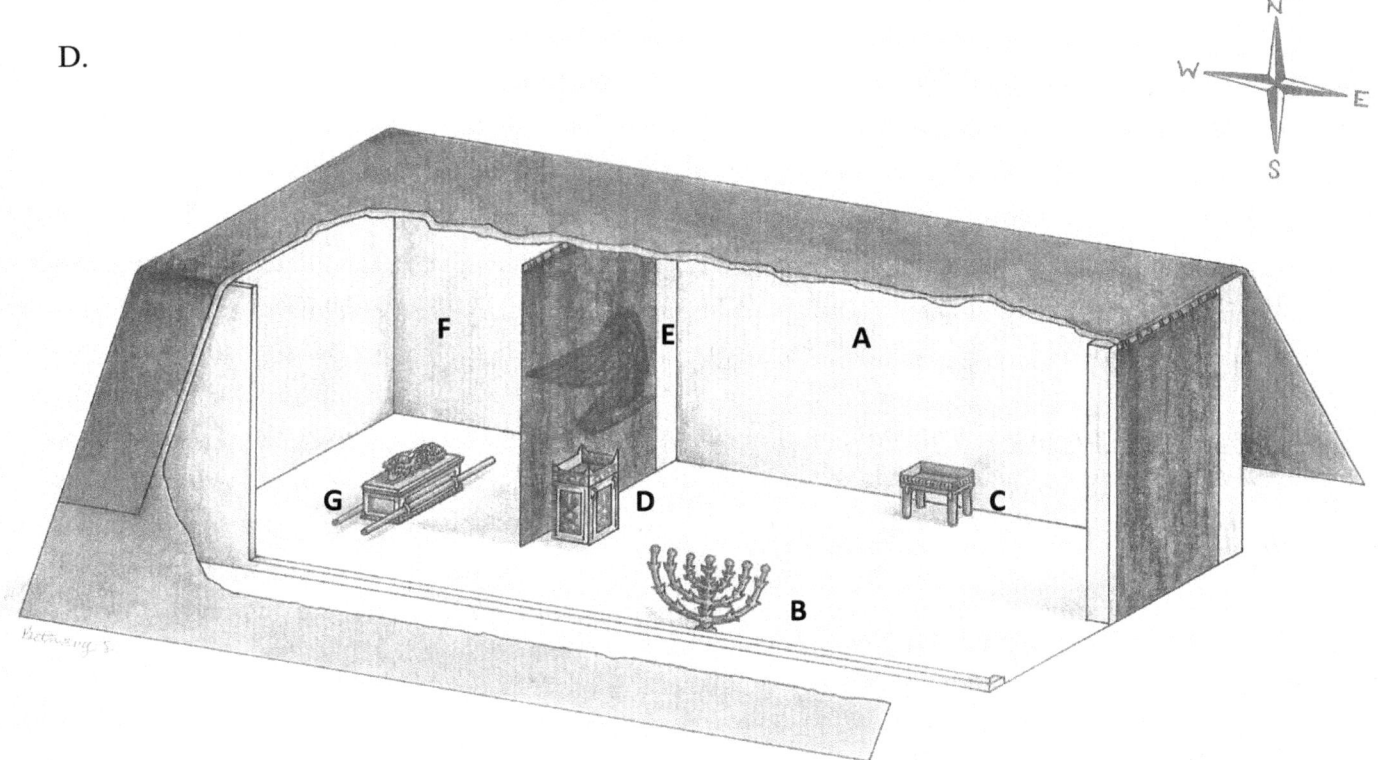

The pastor says "of these things we cannot now speak in detail." His readers would have been very familiar with all the items mentioned and how they were significant in daily worship and special festivals, especially on the Day of Atonement (in Hebrew: Yom Kippur).

You might need a little bit of background information to have a better understanding of these furnishings.

Highlight any comments that represent or communicate the **holiness of God**.

<u>*The Lampstand*</u> *– in Hebrew: "menorah," meaning candlestick, light. It was made of gold and had seven branches with a central stem and 3 branches on either side.* ^{NLT} **Exodus 25:33, 37** Each of the six branches will have three lamp cups shaped like almond blossoms, complete with buds and petals. ³⁷Its lamps are to be set up so they illuminate the area in front of it. *There were no windows inside the tabernacle and the lampstand provided light for the priests as they served inside the first section, called the Holy Place.*

<u>*The Table and Bread*</u> *–* ^{NLT} **Exodus 25:23-24** Then make a table of acacia wood, 36 inches long, 18 inches wide, and 27 inches high. Overlay it with pure gold and run a gold molding around the edge. *The gold-covered wood table had on it the Bread of the Presence (Exodus 25:30): one loaf to represent each of the twelve tribes, placed fresh every Sabbath (Lev. 24:5-9), which only the priests were allowed to eat inside the Holy Place.¹*

<u>*The Second Veil*</u> *– In some translations, called a "curtain," this separated the first section of the tabernacle (the Holy Place) from the inmost section (the Holy of Holies). It was called the second veil to distinguish it from the veil at the entrance to the tabernacle.* ^{NLT} **Exodus 26:31, 33** For the inside of the Tabernacle, make a special curtain of finely woven linen. Decorate it with blue, purple, and scarlet thread and with skillfully embroidered cherubim. Hang the inner curtain from clasps, and put the Ark of the Covenant in the room behind it. This curtain will separate the Holy Place from the Most Holy Place.

<u>*The Altar of Incense*</u> *– This golden altar stood in the Holy Place just in front of the veil that divided the two parts of the tabernacle. It did not stand inside the Holy of Holies, but its ministry pertained to the Holy of Holies.²* ^{NLT} **Exodus 30:6** Place the incense altar just outside the inner curtain that shields the Ark of the Covenant. *The high priest took burning incense from that altar with him into the Holy of Holies so that the smoke of it would cover the mercy seat and protect him from death (Leviticus 16:12-13).³*

The Ark of the Covenant – *This was considered the throne of God in the tabernacle. The cover is called the Mercy Seat. (Atonement cover in the following translation.)* ^{NLT} **Exodus 25:10-11, 16-18, 22** Have the people make an Ark of acacia wood—a sacred chest 45 inches long, 27 inches wide, and 27 inches high. "Overlay it inside and outside with pure gold, and run a molding of gold all around it. ¹⁶When the Ark is finished, place inside it the stone tablets inscribed with the terms of the covenant, which I will give to you. ¹⁷Then make the Ark's cover—the place of atonement—from pure gold. It must be 45 inches long and 27 inches wide. ¹⁸Then make two cherubim from hammered gold, and place them on the two ends of the atonement cover. ²²I will meet with you there and talk to you from above the atonement cover between the gold cherubim that hover over the Ark of the Covenant. From there I will give you my commands for the people of Israel.

> Each year at Yom-Kippur (the Day of Atonement), the high priest would enter the Holy of Holies and drench the top of the Mercy Seat with the blood of the animal sacrificed to make atonement for the people. This was the physical place where the Lord met the high priest on Yom-Kippur (Leviticus 16:2) and where He forgave the sins of the people of Israel. [4]

The Jar of Manna – The Ark of the Covenant held the golden pot that had manna within it as a perpetual reminder of God's faithfulness to provide for His people in their wilderness experience (Exodus 16:33).[5]

Aaron's Rod – The Ark of the Covenant also contained Aaron's rod that budded, a perpetual reminder that God had singled out the tribe of Levi and the house of Aaron as those who would occupy the priestly office (Numbers 17:10).[6]

The Tablets – The Ark of the Covenant contained the tablets on which the Law delivered to Israel had been written, a reminder that God was judging His redeemed people by that Law, holding them responsible for its observance (Exodus 25:16).[7]

The Lord gave precise instructions for all the articles of the tabernacles. Each item is meaningful; each item points toward Jesus; each item was to be treated as holy. Wiersbe says: "No doubt many spiritual truths are wrapped up in these pieces of furniture, and all of them are of value. But the most important truth is this: All of this was symbolism and not the spiritual reality." [8] The pastor briefly mentioned them only as he was making the critical point about the inferiority of the Old Covenant.

What did the priests do according to Hebrews 9:6? Specifically, when did they do this?

Who entered the second part (the Holy of Holies) of the tabernacle, according to Hebrews 9:7?

When did he enter it?

How and why did he enter it?

> The division of the tabernacle into a front and rear compartment was significant, for it indicated that approach to God was not an easy matter. The old sanctuary consisted of a system of barriers between the worshipper and God. The reason for detailing the arrangement of the tabernacle and the furnishings in 9:2-5 is manifestly to show the lack of access to God under the old [system.] [9]

Please read Hebrews 9:1-10 again. Is there anything that the pastor says that disparages the worship set in place by the Lord through the Old Covenant?

What did the pastor tell us in Hebrews 1:1-2?

I love how Guthrie expresses the old way compared to the new:

> The Old Testament revelation is the moon in relationship to the New Covenant sun. In the darkness of the Old Testament era it shone brightly, giving insight to the holy, loving God of the universe, but this true, older light has now been eclipsed by the full intensity of revelation in God's Son. [10]

What revelation and explanation were given by the Holy Spirit according to Hebrews 9:8-10?

> Every detail of the service in the tabernacle was symbolic, foreshadowing through a temporary arrangement that which would be accomplished permanently by Jesus Christ through His death. [11]

This system of worship was set in place by God Himself, and in His wisdom, His requirements showed the inadequacy of the earthly tabernacle, the inadequacy of the Levitical priesthood, and the inadequacy of the Old Covenant.

Note the magnificent statement made by the pastor in Hebrews 9:11:

But _____ came as _____ _____ of the good things to come and entered through the _____ and _____ _____ tabernacle.

We have so very much for which to be thankful. You don't have to be a high priest to enter the presence of God. If you are a follower of Jesus, you can follow Him into the holy presence of God.

What can you do because of what Jesus has done, according to Hebrews 4:16?

Please take time to rejoice, give thanks, and make your requests known to our holy and gracious God.

LESSON 23: ONCE FOR ALL TIME
HEBREWS 9:11-15

The title of this lesson is truly, absolutely wonderful and amazing. Not my use of it, but the truth of it. Once. This is just one of the overwhelming accomplishments of Jesus our High Priest. He entered the greater tabernacle—one time. No other sacrifice or work is necessary to achieve forgiveness of our sins.

We will continue looking at the second movement of the symphony and concentrate on the accomplishment of the sacrifice of Christ. Psalms of lament were played on an eight-stringed lyre. Perhaps this is the instrument that we should imagine being played at this point in the symphony.

2nd Movement: Hebrews 9:1-22
The Sanctuary – Hebrews 9:1-10
Sacrifice – Hebrews 9:11-15
Covenant – Hebrews 9:16-22

Please pray for the enlightenment of the Holy Spirit and to understand the joy of the New Covenant.

Please read Hebrews 9:1-10 to review the situation of the Old Covenant.

Give a brief summary of what we learned in our last lesson about the Old Covenant. What was the importance of it and what was the inadequacy of it?

What part of a person is specifically mentioned in Hebrews 9:9? What was the deficiency of the Old Covenant regarding this part of a person?

How does Titus 1:15 describe the conscience of someone without Christ?

Consider the conscience as described in the verse above. I asked you in a previous lesson: Is a person basically good or basically bad? What does the Bible say?

Is the problem for people an internal or an external one? Did worship through the sacrifices at the tabernacle address the real problem? Reread Hebrews 9:1-10, and please explain your answer.

Look ahead in Hebrews to the difference that Jesus makes through the New Covenant. Note the description of the conscience in:

Hebrews 9:14

Hebrews 10:22

Hebrews 13:18

In the next section of the second movement of the symphony, the pastor will focus on the sacrifice—of the New Covenant.

Please read Hebrews 9:11-15.

These verses present several contrasts between the Old Covenant (the tabernacle and sacrifices) and the New Covenant (the heavenly tabernacle and sacrifice of Christ).

Note the differences below according to Hebrews 9:11-14, also recalling details from Hebrews 9:1-11. Some categories will have notes in both columns.

	Old Covenant	New Covenant
High priest		
Construction of tabernacle		
Offered the Blood of		
Entered the Holy of Holies		
High priest obtained		
Blood of bulls and goats sanctifies		
Blood of Christ cleanses		

What are the eternal, life-changing differences that the New Covenant provides, based on your observations above?

Please read Hebrews 9:11-15 again. What language does the pastor use to communicate the extreme significance of the sacrifice of Christ? What words express the magnitude of Christ's sacrifice?

One of the many remarkable phrases in Hebrews 9:12 is "once for all." This phrase is used in most English translations, and the same phrase is used in Hebrews 7:27 and Hebrews 10:10. It is from one Greek word: ephapax, meaning a single occurrence; a one-time only action; once for all time.

The phrase "once for all" clearly describes Christ's one time sacrifice in comparison to the required yearly sacrifices offered on the Day of Atonement. However, this phrase could be taken out of context and incorrectly interpreted to support the false teaching of universalism, which states that every human will be reconciled to God.

John 1:12 teaches us that Christ's sacrifice makes reconciliation to God possible for all who do what?

You might have made a note of this in a previous answer, but we need to make sure that we don't miss what the pastor emphasized in Hebrews 9:12. How did Christ obtain eternal redemption?

Not with _____ but with _____.

What eternal truth is proclaimed in Leviticus 17:11?

> Not without awe and trembling, and yet with deep and solemn joy, ought a Christian to speak of the precious blood of Christ.[1]

What do the following verses tell us about the blood of Christ?

Matthew 26:28

Acts 20:28

Romans 5:9

Ephesians 2:13

Please contemplate the truths expressed in Hebrews 9:14, by writing this verse in its entirety.

I can only pause. And praise Jesus. "Jesus who died was God, eternal, infinite, and according to the eternal counsel of the triune Godhead, He laid down His life. The Son of God loved me and gave His life for me." [2]

What is your response to Jesus' offering of His life for you?

We've been looking at historical and spiritual and eternal events. Sometimes people wonder what that has to do with us today, right now, as we are paying bills, raising kids, being friends, and living life. Every aspect of our lives should be lived according to the biblical perspective that God created us for His purposes.

What are God's purposes for us, in the verses below?

Ecclesiastes 12:13-14

1 Corinthians 10:31

2 Corinthians 5:10

What was the goal of the cleansing sacrifice of Christ, according to Hebrews 9:14?

Has your conscience been cleansed by the blood of Christ? Are you serving the living God? How does that show up in your everyday life and activities?

LESSON 24: THE PROMISED INHERITANCE
HEBREWS 9:15-22

When I was growing up, my grandmother told me that she was going to give me her silverware, and she was going to give her ring to my sister. It was a precious promise and I enjoyed using the silverware when we visited her house, knowing that it would be mine one day. But it was a sad day when I learned of her death.

The exceedingly precious promise from God of our eternal inheritance was made available to us through the death of His Son. The pastor will make this point clear to his readers in Hebrews 9:15-22.

Please pray that the Holy Spirit will enable you to trust the promises of God.

We are still looking at the second movement of the symphony and now will focus on how the sacrifice of Christ brought about the New Covenant.

2nd Movement: Hebrews 9:1-22
The Sanctuary – Hebrews 9:1-10
Sacrifice – Hebrews 9:11-15
Covenant – Hebrews 9:16-22

Please read Hebrews 9:1-22.

What title is given to Christ in Hebrews 9:15? Why is He given this title?

Please look up the following word:
Mediator – Strong's #3316:
Greek word:
Greek definition:

From the earliest days of history, the Bible shows us that sinful man needed someone to intercede, to help, to speak to God on our behalf. Job longed for a mediator (Job 9:33). We have seen in our study of the tabernacle that the high priest interceded for sinners, but their work was never finished. Did those who sought forgiveness before Jesus' death on the cross receive it?

Consider the following passages and comments below.

What did God promise to Abraham, in Genesis 12:2 and Genesis 17:7-8?

Paul explains a few things about God's covenant with Abraham, especially that it was promised before the Mosaic Law (the Old Covenant) was given; and that it referred specifically to Jesus Christ as the One through whom blessing would come.

Note Paul's statements about "promise" rather than "law", and note the purpose of the law, according to Galatians 3:16-19.

According to Hebrews 8:12, God promised in the New Covenant that: "I will be merciful to their unrighteousness, and their sins and their lawless deeds I will remember no more."

What does Hebrews 9:15 say that parallels the promise of the New Covenant stated above?

The first covenant (Mosaic Law) could never remove moral guilt or the penalty of sin, yet people were saved in the ages before the advent of Christ. God was free to justify repentant sinners because the crucifixion of Christ was divinely viewed as a finished work in the eternal decree of redemption. Christ was the Lamb of God slain before the foundation of the world (1 Peter 1:20; Revelation 13:8), but historically actualized at the cross. He died "for the redemption of the transgressions that were under the first covenant." [1]

I hope that helps you understand God's plan of salvation for those who lived before the time of Christ. He has always saved by grace through faith (Ephesians 2:8-9).

Let's look at the rest of the pastor's comments about covenants and how they are made officially valid.

Please read Hebrews 9:15-22 in the translation below. The NAS uses the most appropriate words to communicate the pastor's intended message.

Highlight, circle, or underline the words **covenant, death,** and **blood.** Make sure you notice the distinction between the New Covenant and the first covenant.

^{NAS} **Hebrews 9:15-22** And for this reason He is the mediator of a new covenant, in order that since a death has taken place for the redemption of the transgressions that were committed under the first covenant, those who have been called may receive the promise of the eternal inheritance. ^{16}For where a covenant is, there must of necessity be the death of the one who made it. ^{17}For a covenant is valid only when men are dead, for it is never in force while the one who made it lives. ^{18}Therefore even the first covenant was not inaugurated without blood. ^{19}For when every commandment had been spoken by Moses to all the people according to the Law, he took the blood of the calves and the goats, with water and scarlet wool and hyssop, and sprinkled both the book itself and all the people, ^{20}saying, "This is the blood of the covenant which God commanded you." ^{21}And in the same way he sprinkled both the tabernacle and all the vessels of the ministry with the blood. ^{22}And according to the Law, one may almost say, all things are cleansed with blood, and without shedding of blood there is no forgiveness.

What death occurred to formalize the first covenant (the Old, Mosaic Covenant)?

What death occurred to formalize the New Covenant?

Which was a greater sacrifice?

Hold fast to Jesus! Everything about Him and everything He has done is far superior to anything, anyone, or any action that has ever or will ever take place. No thing and no one and no other form of worship are better than Jesus and what He provides.

Please take time to reflect on anything or anyone that you might be giving greater honor, devotion, and priority to besides Jesus.

My prayer for us is that we will understand the important truths spoken through the pastor. But I'd like to remind you that our goal is not just to gain knowledge. My prayer is that the truths we study will be connected between our heads and our hearts.

Hebrews 9:15 is a rich summary of the accomplishment of Jesus as our High Priest. Using phrases from this verse, write a prayer of thanksgiving for what He has done.

LESSON 25: DO YOU WANT TO GO TO HEAVEN?
HEBREWS 9:23-28

A popular theme of fictional stories and movies is for a character to experience an alternate reality. A mother and daughter wish to change places with each other. A little boy just wants to be big. A desperate man wishes he had never been born. Then all of a sudden, something out of the ordinary happens, and like Alice in Wonderland, they "fall down the rabbit hole" into a completely different life experience.

*Where am I going with this?! We need to realize that Heaven is not a fictional, alternate reality. And neither is this life. This is real. And Heaven is real. But life on earth, as beautiful, colorful, and fascinating as it is, is only a dull, shadowy experience compared to the brilliant, extraordinary, better reality of Heaven. And what **makes** Heaven – Heaven? God.*

The passage we will study today will teach us about things of the earth and the better things of Heaven. But more importantly, it will teach us about the better sacrifice of Christ and what it provided for those who trust Him as their Savior.

Please pray that you will believe the word of God and trust the Holy Spirit for assurance of your salvation.

Just to remind you of the outline we are following, we have come to the third movement of the symphony.

3rd Movement: Hebrews 9:23-10:18
The Sanctuary – Hebrews 9:23-24
Sacrifice – Hebrews 9:25-10:14
Covenant – Hebrews 10:15-18

Please read Hebrews 8:1-9:27. We need the review and we need to follow the train of thought as the pastor makes his points.

What crucial view of the earthly tabernacle are we reminded of in Hebrews 9:23-24?

Note the details from the verses below that support this truth.

Hebrews 8:5

Hebrews 9:1

Hebrews 9:9

How is heaven described in Hebrews 9:24?

How is the heavenly tabernacle described in the following verses?

Hebrews 8:2

Hebrews 9:8

Hebrews 9:11

Hebrews 9:12

The pastor tells his readers that "it was necessary" that the earthly tabernacle and its furnishings be purified with the blood of bulls and goats (Hebrews 9:22-23). It was necessary because it represented the holiness of God, and the earthly tabernacle symbolized the way to have fellowship with our holy God. As we have seen in our study so far, access and approach to God was not an easy matter. There was a barrier, represented by the veils and the sections of the tabernacle.

The barrier to access to God was then and is now—sin.

"And without the shedding of blood there is no _____ ." Hebrews 9:22

Have you ever been wronged? Cheated against? Slandered? Stolen from? This is the way we have treated God and it is sin against Him even if you are normally a nice person!

Do you want to go to Heaven? You can't, if your sin is blocking the way. But there is hope!

Jesus Christ removed the barrier for us. Incredible truths are made clear in Hebrews 9:24-26.

Fill in the blanks below as you observe His amazing, perfect sacrifice.

Hebrews 9:24: Christ has entered into _____ _____, to appear in the _____ of God, for _____.

Hebrews 9:25: He did not enter to offer Himself _____.

Hebrews 9:26: But _____, He appeared to do away with _____ by the _____ of _____.

The pastor makes a logical argument for the superiority of Jesus' work. He compares the earthly tabernacle to the heavenly tabernacle. He compares the unending work of the Levitical high priest to the one-time work of Jesus the High Priest. And he compares the sacrifice of animals to the sacrifice of Jesus the sinless, self-less Man.

> The pastor has chosen his words carefully in order to describe the complete destruction of sin by Christ. Sin is no longer in force and thus no longer determines the lives of its once-victims. This removal of sin dominates the history of the world, for it has happened once for all at the climax of history and will need no further attention even at Christ's return.[1]

Where is Jesus right now, according to Hebrews 8:1 and 9:24?

Please read Hebrews 9:23-24 again.

You might be wondering, why do the "heavenly things" need cleansing?"

> If sin erected a barrier forbidding entrance into the sanctuary that was a "pattern," how much more did it bar the way into the "true" Sanctuary in which God dwells.[2]

*We need to understand that the problem is sin. Sin is the barrier. Sin had to be dealt with. And that is just what Jesus did. He did what the Levitical high priests could not do. He offered Himself as **one** sacrifice, **one time**, and bore the judgment for sin **once**.*

What sobering truth does Hebrews 9:27 tell us?

Now look at the corresponding statement in the next verse. Hebrews 9:28 tells us that just as a person dies once, so also Christ _____ to bear the sins of many.

A contrast is also presented between Hebrews 9:27 and 9:28. A person faces judgment after death. But Christ died once and will appear again, not to face judgment, not to be sacrificed for sin, but instead to bring salvation.

Life on earth is real. Death comes to all men. Life after death is real. Judgment awaits all men.

Are you prepared to die? Why or why not?

Let's briefly look at a few verses regarding life after death, resurrection, and the types of judgment that are ahead. Note what you learn in the following verses.

Daniel 12:2

John 5:28-29

Acts 24:15

1 Corinthians 15:20-22

2 Corinthians 5:10

Revelation 20:11-15

I hope that you can see from the verses above that there are two types of judgment after death. One is for those who have trusted in Christ as their Savior. It's called the "judgment seat of Christ" (2 Cor. 5:10) and is a place of reward for faithful good works of a believer, not judgment of sin. The other is called the Great White Throne judgment for those who have rejected Christ and His salvation (Rev. 20:11-15).

We could spend much more time on this topic, but I hope that you grasp the certainty of death and the certainty of judgment.

Hebrews 2:15 tells us that Christ came to deliver us from the fear of death. What are we to eagerly anticipate, instead of fear, according to Hebrews 9:28? (Note **who** and **what**.)

On the Day of Atonement, the people eagerly awaited the appearance of the high priest after he presented the sacrifice in the Holy of Holies. His "second appearance" signified that his sacrifice had been accepted by God. His reappearance was a joyful occasion!

> Christ's second coming to bring final salvation for His people is the ultimate proof that His sacrifice was once for all, and unrepeatable because it is absolutely sufficient.[3]

We have studied biblical truths that have eternal consequences. There is no alternate reality.

Life and death, sin and judgment, Heaven and salvation — are all real.

What is your view of sin? How does it impact the way you live your life?

What is your view of Heaven? How does it impact the way you live your life?

What is your view of death? How does it impact the way you live your life?

What is your view of judgment? How does it impact the way you live your life?

What is your view of the return of Christ? How does it impact the way you live your life?

The anticipation of Christ's return and His salvation is quite the motivation for perseverance through the trials of this life.

LESSON 26: THE SACRIFICE OF CHRIST
HEBREWS 10:1-14

How do you feel about music? Can you take it or leave it? Or maybe you've got to have it! Do you listen to music that mirrors your emotions? It's interesting to consider how important music is in movies. Some songs make a movie great. There once was a day when movies had very little music in the background of dramatic scenes. Those movies seem quite flat and boring compared to the ones whose music perfectly supports the moments of drama, action, humor or suspense.

In this lesson, we will listen to the climax of the third movement of the symphony. This is the point of the greatest crescendo and emphasis as the pastor expounds more than before on the sacrifice of Jesus Christ. If orchestral, symphonic music isn't your style, please consider it to be the most meaningful, exciting highlight of your favorite song.

Please pray that you will hear the message of the Holy Spirit and respond in faith and thanksgiving.

Please look at the outline that we've been following and notice the number of verses in each section:

	First Movement	**Second Movement**	**Third Movement**
Sanctuary	Hebrews 8:1-2	Hebrews 9:1-10	Hebrews 9:23-24
Sacrifice	Hebrews 8:3-6	Hebrews 9:11-15	Hebrews 9:25-10:14
Covenant	Hebrews 8:7-13	Hebrews 9:16-22	Hebrews 10:15-18

Circle the topic and the passage that represents the center of the third movement.

> When the author as conductor has finished his symphony, he would leave his hearers overwhelmed with the magnitude and wonder of this High Priest and ready at all cost to persevere through the benefits He affords.[1]

I hope the comments so far have helped prepare you for our study. In our last lesson, we considered the first verses pertaining to Christ's sacrifice. Let's continue now.

Please read Hebrews 9:23-10:14. I've emphasized the quote from Psalms 40:7-9. **Highlight, circle or underline** the words **"sacrifice(s)"** and **"offer(s)(ed), offering(s)"** throughout the entire passage. You don't need to use different colors.

HCSB Hebrews 9:23 - 10:14 Therefore it was necessary for the copies of the things in the heavens to be purified with these sacrifices, but the heavenly things themselves to be purified with better sacrifices than these. ²⁴For the Messiah did not enter a sanctuary made with hands (only a model of the true one) but into heaven itself, that He might now appear in the presence of God for us. ²⁵ He did not do this to offer Himself many times, as the high priest enters the sanctuary yearly with the blood of another. ²⁶ Otherwise, He would have had to suffer many times since the foundation of the world. But now He has appeared one time, at the end of the ages, for the removal of sin by the sacrifice of Himself. ²⁷ And just as it is appointed for people to die once—and after this, judgment— ²⁸ so also the Messiah, having been offered once to bear the sins of many, will appear a second time, not to bear sin, but to bring salvation to those who are waiting for Him. **Hebrews 10:1** Since the law has only a shadow of the good things to come, and not the actual form of those realities, it can never perfect the worshipers by the same sacrifices they continually offer year after year. ² Otherwise, wouldn't they have stopped being offered, since the worshipers, once purified, would no longer have any consciousness of sins? ³ But in the sacrifices there is a reminder of sins every year. ⁴ For it is impossible for the blood of bulls and goats to take away sins. ⁵ Therefore, as He was coming into the world, He said:

You did not want sacrifice and offering, but You prepared a body for Me.
⁶ You did not delight in whole burnt offerings and sin offerings.
⁷ Then I said, "See, I have come—it is written about Me in the volume of the scroll—
to do Your will, O God!"

⁸ After He says above,

You did not desire or delight in sacrifices and offerings,
whole burnt offerings and sin offerings,

(which are offered according to the law), ⁹ He then says,

See, I have come to do Your will.

He takes away the first to establish the second. ¹⁰ By this will, we have been sanctified through the offering of the body of Jesus Christ once and for all. ¹¹ Now every priest stands day after day ministering and offering time after time the same sacrifices, which can never take away sins. ¹² But this man, after offering one sacrifice for sins forever, sat down at the right hand of God. ¹³ He is now waiting until His enemies are made His footstool. ¹⁴ For by one offering He has perfected forever those who are sanctified.

According to Hebrews 10:1-4, what were the problems with the law (the Old Covenant system of sacrifices and priesthood)?

In Hebrews 10:2-3, what evidence does the pastor give that emphasizes that the Old Covenant did not bring about God's desired goal for people?

Please highlight the word "therefore" in Hebrews 10:5 and read Hebrews 10:4-7.

> Christ came as a superior high priest and brought a superior offering. The use of "therefore" shows that the inability of the law's sacrificial system is set in stark contrast to the offering of Christ.[2]

Who is speaking in Hebrews 10:5? See Hebrews 9:24 and 28 for the antecedent of the pronoun.

When did He say it, according to Hebrews 10:5?

The quotation of Psalm 40:7-9 is fascinating, presented as the very words of Christ. The pastor understood these verses as being fulfilled by Jesus when He came to earth as a man.

The pastor is giving us insight into the commitment of the Son of God just as He was about to enter life on earth. Wow. One commentator says this was spoken by Jesus on the "eve of His incarnation." [3] *That's Christmas Eve, to me. Or perhaps, just before the Virgin Mary was overshadowed by the power of God and Christ was conceived.*

What phrase in Hebrews 10:5 refers to God sending Jesus to earth as a man?

It is so precious and amazing to think about this miracle. Please enjoy the verses below and note truths about the profound mystery of God giving His Eternal Son a body of flesh and blood.

Matthew 1:20-23

Luke 1:35

Galatians 4:4

1 Timothy 3:16

Here in Hebrews, the psalm presents the obedience of Jesus Christ and His resolute intention to carry out the will of God by giving His body on the cross as the perfect sacrifice for sins.

What similar ideas are presented in Philippians 2:5-8?

Just in case you are one of those with an inquiring mind who wants to know more about background details, here is a brief comment on the wording of Psalm 40:6-8:

> The psalm is quoted from the Septuagint version (Greek Old Testament), in which the Hebrew words "my ears you have opened" are given the interpretive paraphrase: "a body you have prepared for me." The Greek translators evidently regarded the Hebrew wording as an instance of a part (ears) taken for the whole (body).[4]

Please read Hebrews 10:5-9. What is more important to the Lord than burnt offerings and sacrifices?

The Lord always desired heartfelt devotion rather than empty rituals. Note the Lord's will as expressed in the following verses:

1 Samuel 15:22

Ecclesiastes 5:1

Jeremiah 7:22-23

Micah 6:6-8

Mark 12:33

Do you delight to do the will of God? Is there hypocrisy in your worship of the Lord? Consider whether your actions, service, and words represent an honest heartfelt devotion to the Lord. Is there anything in which you are just going through the motions?

Please record the words of Psalm 40:8-9, from which the pastor has quoted.

The Old Testament that we now hold as a leather-bound book or read on an electronic device was once written on parchment—the scraped, dried, and stretched skin of animals. Pages were glued together side by side and rolled, forming a scroll which could be referred to as a book.

There is no doubt that Jesus delighted in obeying the instructions of the Lord and that He also knew that the Scriptures pointed to Him. He obeyed God's Word and fulfilled the promises of God's Word.

What did Jesus say about the Scriptures in Luke 24:25-27 and Luke 24:44-45?

The sacrifice of Christ was acceptable to God because He wanted to obey the will of God and He submitted Himself completely to the will of God. Everything about the sacrifice of Christ was better than the sacrifices and offerings of the Old Covenant. Animals had no choice in the matter. Animals couldn't offer themselves. Animals didn't substitute themselves for all mankind. But the unblemished lambs offered at Passover were symbolic of the Lamb of God who offered Himself and took away the sins of the world.

Let's end today's lesson with thanksgiving for the truth repeated in Hebrews 10:10 and 14. What happened through the one-time offering of the body of Christ?

There is so much to celebrate. What we needed and what God wanted was provided. Once for all time.

We'll hear the conclusion to the glorious symphony in the next lesson.

LESSON 27: A Total Transformation
Hebrews 10:9-17

We've been immersed in the main message of the pastor for many lessons. He gave us an introduction to Jesus as our High Priest in Hebrews 4:14-16. He then focused on the superiority of Jesus in every way in Hebrews 5:1-10:18, explaining His priesthood, His sacrifice, and His obedience.

We've seen the final section of the pastor's teaching described as a symphony in three movements and the music swelled at the end with the grandeur of the sacrifice of Christ. We touched on the achievement of His offering in the last lesson, but now we will examine it more closely. The promise of the total transformation through the New Covenant was fulfilled through Jesus' sacrifice.

Please pray that you will receive the teaching of the Holy Spirit and respond with your whole heart and mind.

In Lesson 21 we briefly looked at the promises of the New Covenant. We've focused mainly on the inadequacies of the Old (Mosaic) Covenant. It will be exciting to focus on the superior New Covenant now.

Please read Hebrews 8:6-13 and Hebrews 10:9-18 below. Highlight the ideas of **(1) more excellent, better; (2) old, first; (3) new, second.** I've underlined the specifics of the New Covenant in each passage, where the author quoted Jeremiah 31:33-34.

ESV **Hebrews 8:6-13** But as it is, Christ has obtained a ministry that is as much more excellent than the old as the covenant he mediates is better, since it is enacted on better promises. ⁷For if that first covenant had been faultless, there would have been no occasion to look for a second. ⁸For he finds fault with them when he says: "Behold, the days are coming, declares the Lord, when I will establish a new covenant with the house of Israel and with the house of Judah, ⁹not like the covenant that I made with their fathers on the day when I took them by the hand to bring them out of the land of Egypt. For they did not continue in my covenant, and so I showed no concern for them, declares the Lord. ¹⁰<u>For this is the covenant that I will make with the house of Israel after those days, declares the Lord: I will put my</u>

laws into their minds, and write them on their hearts, and I will be their God, and they shall be my people. "And they shall not teach, each one his neighbor and each one his brother, saying, 'Know the Lord,' for they shall all know me, from the least of them to the greatest. ¹²For I will be merciful toward their iniquities, and I will remember their sins no more." ¹³In speaking of a new covenant, he makes the first one obsolete. And what is becoming obsolete and growing old is ready to vanish away.

Hebrews 10:9-18 Then he added, "Behold, I have come to do your will." He abolishes the first in order to establish the second. ¹⁰And by that will we have been sanctified through the offering of the body of Jesus Christ once for all. ¹¹And every priest stands daily at his service, offering repeatedly the same sacrifices, which can never take away sins. ¹²But when Christ had offered for all time a single sacrifice for sins, he sat down at the right hand of God, ¹³waiting from that time until his enemies should be made a footstool for his feet. ¹⁴For by a single offering he has perfected for all time those who are being sanctified. ¹⁵And the Holy Spirit also bears witness to us; for after saying, ¹⁶ "This is the covenant that I will make with them after those days, declares the Lord: I will put my laws on their hearts, and write them on their minds," ¹⁷then he adds, "I will remember their sins and their lawless deeds no more." ¹⁸Where there is forgiveness of these, there is no longer any offering for sin.

What were the inadequacies of the Old Covenant, according to Hebrews 8:9 and Hebrews 10:11?

What are the wonderful benefits of the New Covenant, according to Hebrews 8:10 and 12?

These benefits are further explained and emphasized in the pastor's conclusion:

Hebrews 10:10: We have been _____ through the offering of the body of Jesus Christ _____

Hebrews 10:14: He has perfected _____ those who are being _____

Hebrews 10:16: . . . Declares the Lord: I will put _____ on their _____ and write them on their _____

Hebrews 10:17: . . . Then He adds: I will remember their _____ and lawless deeds _____

The pastor repeated these extraordinary truths for emphasis. Reading, rereading, and writing them out for ourselves helps us meditate on, remember and understand them. This is critical information that truly describes salvation and the life of a Christian. It is also the reason that the pastor will urge his readers to persevere in their faith through the trials of life.

Jesus has made it possible for us to live the life God wants us to live. The New Covenant makes the way for the transformation of the heart and mind and shows us that God desires a relationship with us, not just obedience to rules and rituals.

Please summarize the total transformation of our lives that the New Covenant provides, based on the passages above and questions you have answered.

Please look up the definition for the following word:
Sanctified: Strong's #37
Greek word:
Greek definition:

The first time that word is used in this passage (Hebrews 10:10), it is a perfect passive participle. The perfect tense of Greek verbs indicates that the action which took place continues to have an effect.

The second time that word is used in the passage (Hebrews 10:14), it is a present passive participle, indicating that the action is occurring at the present time.

Even if you don't like grammar, please rejoice in what these two verb tenses indicate! Jesus' sacrifice removed the sin that was the barrier between us and God, and His work lasts forever.

> This perfecting is of such a quality that it will never need renewal or supplementation. Nothing more need be done for God's people to be delivered from sin and brought into God's presence.[1]

What did the pastor say about standing and sitting, in Hebrews 10:11-13? How does this relate to the comment above?

Is there anything that you are doing to try to add to the finished work of Christ?

We've seen that the obedience of Jesus, the Son of God, Son of Man, made possible the fulfillment of the New Covenant. His offering, the shedding of His blood, met the requirement needed for forgiveness of sins. He paid the price to validate the New Covenant. But what was the action that brought about the terms of the New Covenant? What happens to a person so that the promise of the New Covenant can be fulfilled in them? The answer is found in the prophecy made through Ezekiel.

What action does God Himself take to bring about the terms of the New Covenant, according to Ezekiel 36:22, 25-27?

What, or Who, specifically, brings about the transformation promised in the New Covenant, according to Ezekiel 36:27?

How do the following verses echo this promise?
Galatians 5:16

Ephesians 3:16

2 Thessalonians 2:13

Titus 3:4-6

What is the relief that we have because of this total transformation, according to Romans 8:1-4?

Do you remember the main point the pastor was making? I emphasized the beginning of his message with capital letters, underlining, and exclamation points. We need to see the first notes of his symphony in coordination with his last notes which also need to be emphasized with capital letters. This is a big deal! Drumroll, please . . . .

^{NKJ} HEBREWS 8:1
NOW THIS IS THE MAIN POINT OF THE THINGS WE ARE SAYING:
WE HAVE SUCH A HIGH PRIEST,
WHO IS SEATED AT THE RIGHT HAND
OF THE THRONE OF THE MAJESTY IN THE HEAVENS!

^{ESV} HEBREWS 10:17-18
I WILL REMEMBER THEIR SINS AND THEIR LAWLESS DEEDS NO MORE. ¹⁸WHERE THERE IS FORGIVENESS OF THESE, THERE IS NO LONGER ANY OFFERING FOR SIN!

I would love to have heard the pastor preach his sermon! I imagine that he would have passionately explained the priestly work of Jesus. It isn't stuffy ancient history.

What is your reaction to all that we have studied?

What was Paul's reaction to it, according to 2 Corinthians 3:7-9?

Oh! The glory of it all! If you're happy and you know it, then your face will surely show it! Let thankfulness make you smile and shine!

LESSON 28: UNRESTRICTED ACCESS
Hebrews 10:19-25

What is the furthest distance or longest time you've been away from your loved ones? Have you experienced the pain of homesickness? The longing to be back with the one you love? I remember staying at my grandmother's as a child and missing my mother so badly. And living hours apart while dating my husband—we had big phone bills! As a parent, I've been on trips without my children and they were on my mind all the time. Now I'm a grandmother myself and am always eager to see my precious little granddaughter!

God loves you. He wants you to be close to Him. And through Christ, He made the way for you to be in His presence any time and all the time. Everything that we've been studying in Hebrews has really been leading up to this great truth. It's not just a fact; it's a passionate urging from the pastor to his readers.

Please pray that you will respond to the loving words of the Lord.

Please look at the verses quoted at the end of the last lesson and read the main point the pastor has made in Hebrews 8:1 and Hebrews 10:17-18. I've emphasized it with capital letters.

Now read Hebrews 10:19-25.

Therefore! The main point has a consequence on our lives! The main point that the pastor has spent so much time on—the accomplishment of our great High Priest Jesus—is to be believed and received.

The pastor has done everything he can to explain the magnitude of Christ's position as our Great High Priest and the work that He has completed. And now the pastor will do everything he can to urge us to respond in the right way to what has been done for us.

What two things do we have, according to Hebrews 10:19-20?

What are we allowed to do because of these things, according to Hebrews 10:19-20?

As I am reflecting on Hebrews 10:19, I am considering the possibility of it being the most magnificent, amazing statement in all of Scripture. Wow. Don't forget that since the time of Adam, free access to the presence of God has been prohibited. Not even the Israelite high priests had unrestricted privileges to enter the Holy of Holies.

Can you see the gospel message in Hebrews 10:19? How does this verse relate to the sin of man, the holiness of God, and the result of Christ's sacrifice?

We can further explain the gospel message through the next verse. Let's look at the key words.

^{NKJ} **Hebrews 10:20** ...by a **new** and **living way** which **He consecrated** for us, through the **veil**, that is, **His flesh**.

New Way: Based on what we've studied in all of Hebrews so far, why is it called a new way?

Living Way: It leads to life in the presence of our _____ Hebrews 10:31

It is a way guaranteed by Jesus who is _____ John 14:6

It is a way guaranteed by Jesus who _____ Hebrews 7:24

Consecrated: Strong's #1457
Greek word:
Greek definition:

^{ESV} **1 Kings 8:63** Solomon offered as peace offerings to the LORD 22,000 oxen and 120,000 sheep. So the king and all the people of Israel dedicated the house of the LORD.

The word used here, consecrate, would have reminded the Hebrew readers of the very special and sacred ceremonies of the dedications of the tabernacle and Solomon's temple. The pastor will continue to show parallels to worship according to the Old Covenant while showing that Jesus provides a brand new and better way.

Veil: Also translated as "curtain." What did this refer to in Hebrews 6:19-20? See page 110 for more information.

His flesh: How do Hebrews 5:7-9 and Luke 23:46 describe this?

Jesus did what no one could do on their own! Jesus did what no high priest could do. Jesus did a brand new thing, for us, through giving His own perfect life as the unblemished sacrifice needed to atone for our sins. And the way is open to all who follow Him.

As we are handling Scripture, I don't want to get bogged down in difficult interpretations, but I do want to mention questions that arise. The phrase "through the veil, that is, His flesh" is considered confusing in Greek and English. Did the author mean that the veil should be understood as Jesus' flesh? It gets very complicated to think through all the possibilities of interpretations of this verse. Feel free to research it on your own.

Here's how I understand it after my research: Jesus made a new and living way for us to enter through the veil of the heavenly tabernacle into the presence of God. That way was made possible through the offering of His flesh. The way is through the veil, that is, through His flesh.

Therefore! We are still actually thinking about the impact of Christ's work. What does the pastor urge us to do?

Read Hebrews 10:22-24 and note the 3 exhortations. (You'll fill in the blanks in the next exercise.)

_____ 1. Let us –

_____ 2. Let us –

_____ 3. Let us –

Look back at each exhortation and note in the blanks above the characteristic that is referred to, for example, in verse 22: full assurance of _____.

When we've received the grace of God through Christ, then we receive faith, hope, and love. And that gives us peace. And that gives us joy!

What a privilege and delight it is to draw near to the Lord. Why does the pastor urge his readers to draw near? He's telling them to do something they weren't doing already. Draw near, don't turn away! Don't drift. Don't neglect your salvation. Don't look anywhere else!

Highlight in the verses below the precious benefits we receive when we draw near to the Lord.

^{ESV} **Hebrews 4:16** Let us then with confidence draw near to the throne of grace, that we may receive mercy and find grace to help in time of need.

^{ESV} **Hebrews 7:25** Consequently, He is able to save to the uttermost those who draw near to God through Him, since He always lives to make intercession for them.

Look at Hebrews 10:22 and describe the condition of our hearts and lives that allow us to draw near to our holy God.

Please record the desires, delights, and blessings of drawing near to the Lord, according to the verses below.

Psalm 16:11

Psalm 73:28

Acts 3:19

James 4:8

And as we noted above, we are to draw near in full assurance of **faith.** *We've already seen the great danger of unbelief. The pastor will repeatedly highlight the critical importance of faith for the rest of his letter.*

Please take time now to enjoy the open access you have into the holy, holy throne room of God. Be with Him. Share your heart with Him. Listen to Him. I pray that you will have full assurance of faith that you are with Him and He is with you.

LESSON 29: HOLD FAST TO HOPE
Hebrews 10:23

I've had the countries of Denmark and Norway on my mind a lot lately. I don't know much about them, but my son and his family are living there for 6 months, so I've become very interested in their new hometown. By the time this book is in print, I will have visited them. And I will have experienced first-hand the seafaring cultures from which much of our English nautical terminology originates. Like "hold fast."

I'm very excited about studying Hebrews 10:23 where Paul urges us to hold fast to the confession of our hope.

Please pray that you will hold tightly to the word of the Lord and trust the Holy Spirit to give you a firm grasp of the truth.

Please write out Hebrews 10:23.

Depending on your translation, you may have written: hold fast, hold on, hold tightly, hold unswervingly, or hold unwaveringly.

The Greek word translated as hold fast is "katecho." When we first studied this word as used in Hebrews 3:6, we learned that it is a nautical term meaning "to hold one's course toward, head for, steer for." The Urban Dictionary says that hold fast means "to bear down, grit it out, stay the course." It was originally a Norwegian nautical term referring to the importance of securely gripping a ship's rigging.[1]

Before studying Hebrews, the phrase "hold fast" was not a normal part of my vocabulary. But you know it is in the title of the study and now it is a very important concept. When I read, hear, or think about this phrase, I think of a ship in a storm with the captain commanding his crew to: Hold Fast! Hold the lines! Hold her steady!

Sailors hold the ropes of the sails to keep a ship on course. What we hold fast is the most important thing about the pastor's exhortation.

What does the pastor tell us to hold on to in the following verses?

Hebrews 3:6 (note 2 things)

Hebrews 3:14

Hebrews 4:14

Hebrews 6:18

While different words are used, the idea communicated in the verses above is basically the same as that in Hebrews 10:23. Let us hold fast to the confession of our hope. Confession here does not mean an acknowledgment of sin, but rather it means "a statement of allegiance expressing binding assent and public commitment."[2]

What must be publicly confessed and believed in your heart, according to Romans 10:9?

What must be publicly acknowledged, according to Matthew 10:32-33?

What should we understand that our confession of hope is based on, according to these verses?

Luke 8:15

1 Corinthians 15:2

1 Thessalonians 5:21

The pastor writing to his beloved flock wants them to hold fast to the truth they have received about Jesus. In Hebrews 10:23, hope is a noun. Not a verb. Even though it is our expectation, it is our present possession because Jesus has accomplished the work that gives us hope. And so, we can sum it all up by saying hold fast to Jesus! He is our hope.

There are so many statements of hope in this letter. Write a few verses from the list below which best express your confession of hope.

Hebrews 2:11

Hebrews 4:9

Hebrews 4:16

Hebrews 6:19-20

Hebrews 7:26-27

Hebrews 8:1-2

Hebrews 9:14

Hebrews 9:24

Hebrews 9:28

Hebrews 10:14

Hebrews 10:16-17

I wonder if you are surprised by some of the previous verses. We usually think of our hope as the glories of heaven and the unspeakable joy we will have when we see our Savior face to face. Oh yes! That is our hope. But we have that hope because of Jesus. If we don't hold fast to Jesus and the work that He has accomplished for us, then we aren't depending on Him for our eternal salvation or our daily difficulties.

> The confession of Christ's full adequacy is, above all things, an affirmation of trust in that assured hope of glory at His return.[3]

Please put the confession of your hope in your own words. Finish the statement:

I'm holding fast to –

We can persevere through daily difficulties because we can draw near to the One who is seated on the throne in heaven. We can find strength and grace from Him in our times of need.

What should be our attitude, based on 2 Corinthians 4:17-18?

Why can we be so certain of the hope that we have for today and for the future? What is the guarantee of our hope according to Hebrews 10:23?

It's a simple statement to make if you believe it. I know the trials of life can sometimes make it feel like God is not faithful. But He is. Always. When circumstances in life don't seem to match the truth of God's Word, please remember: God is faithful.

The confession of our hope is dependent on the declaration of the Lord. What He says, we can believe.

How does the Lord describe Himself in Exodus 34:6?

The Hebrew word "chesed" in the verse above is translated as lovingkindness, steadfast love, loyal love, and faithfulness. A very important aspect of this word is that of faithful commitment. Our God keeps His word.

Moses is the one who heard the Lord directly and quoted Him in Exodus 34:6. Remember that Moses didn't have an easy job leading the grumbling Israelites through the desert for 40 years.

How did he then describe the Lord in the verses below?

Deuteronomy 4:31

Deuteronomy 7:9

The prophet Jeremiah grieved after the destruction of Jerusalem and the Lord's Temple, but what gave him hope, according to Lamentations 3:21-23?

The Hebrews to whom the pastor was writing were suffering. Their circumstances were hard because they were being persecuted for their faith. This will be made clear in upcoming verses. But it was no excuse for turning away from the Lord. Rather, it's all the more reason to hold fast to Jesus. The pastor is about to expound upon the faith we must have and it's all based on the great faithfulness of our God.

Are you suffering? If yes, then I am so sorry for the pain and difficulty in your life. You are not alone.

As you hold fast to Jesus, know that He is holding fast to you.

Write out the precious truths from the verses below.

Psalm 73:23-25

Psalm 139:9-10

When life is full of troubled waters, and even when it's nice smooth sailing, our life preserver is Jesus Christ. I'll end this lesson with the following verses from Psalm 107 and the Navy Hymn.

^{NAS} **Psalm 107:23-31** ²³Those who go down to the sea in ships, who do business on great waters; ²⁴they have seen the works of the LORD, and His wonders in the deep. ²⁵For He spoke and raised up a stormy wind, which lifted up the waves of the sea. ²⁶They rose up to the heavens, they went down to the depths; their soul melted away

in their misery. ²⁷They reeled and staggered like a drunken man, and were at their wits' end. ²⁸Then they cried to the LORD in their trouble, and He brought them out of their distresses. ²⁹He caused the storm to be still, so that the waves of the sea were hushed. ³⁰Then they were glad because they were quiet; so He guided them to their desired haven. ³¹Let them give thanks to the LORD for His lovingkindness, and for His wonders to the sons of men!

> "Eternal Father, Strong to Save" is a hymn written by William Whiting in 1860 inspired by the dangers of the sea described in Psalm 107. This hymn is commonly associated with seafarers, particularly in the naval armed services, and is often referred to as the "Navy Hymn." This hymn also has a long tradition in civilian maritime settings and is regularly called upon by ship's chaplains and sung during services on ocean travels.[4]

Eternal Father, strong to save,
Whose arm does bind the restless wave,
Who bids the mighty ocean deep
Its own appointed limits keep;
O hear us when we cry to Thee
For those in peril on the sea.

O Savior, whose almighty word
The winds and waves submissive heard,
Who walked upon the foaming deep,
And calm amid the rage did sleep;
O hear us when we cry to Thee
For those in peril on the sea.

O Holy Spirit, who did brood
Upon the waters dark and rude,
And bid their angry tumult cease,
And give for wild confusion peace;
O hear us when we cry to Thee
For those in peril on the sea.

O Trinity of love and pow'r,
Your children shield in danger's hour;
From rock and tempest, fire, and foe,
Protect them where-so-e'er they go;
Thus, evermore shall rise to Thee
Glad hymns of praise from land and sea.[5]

LESSON 30: Team Spirit
Hebrews 10:24-25

I need you. You need me. God made us that way! He made us for relationship, with Him, and with each other. Even when we are introverted and independent, and especially when we are isolated or in trouble, we need each other. I think that might be why there are so many clubs and groups and sports fans and hashtags! #wareagle #gotigers #auburnalumni

If you don't understand those hashtags, you're probably not from my sweet home Alabama, where I grew up cheering for the Auburn Tigers. I'm a loyal fan who lived on campus and graduated from the university. Football is a big deal in Alabama. But Auburn isn't always a winning team. I say "War Eagle!" anyway. We keep rooting for our team no matter what.

Back to the Bible . . . the pastor writing his friends is cheering them on. Urging them not to give up in the midst of their hardships. Let's listen closely to his counsel.

Please pray that the Holy Spirit will encourage you to hold fast to Jesus and His word.

Please read Hebrews 10:19-23.

Who has our focus been on as we have studied these verses over the last few lessons? What actions have we been urged to take?

Compare Hebrews 10:24-25 with the previous verses, Hebrews 10:19-23, and answer the following questions:

Who is our focus on now?

What are we to do?

What problem is the pastor confronting?

Good job! I'm sure you answered those questions appropriately. This verse is quite familiar to me, and perhaps to you. It is so important.

> Christians have a high calling to care for one another and stimulate one another spiritually and morally. The word translated "let us consider" (katanoeo), means to notice, consider, pay attention to, look closely at.
>
> Believers are to rivet their attention on the need for conscious activities of encouragement among those in the Christian community.[1]

Did you realize that it is a high calling to pay attention to your brothers and sisters in Christ? What is your reaction to this?

For a reminder of a few basic teachings, please note the instructions in the following verses:

Mark 12:29-31

John 15:12-13

Romans 12:10-13

The pastor has urged us to draw near to the Lord in faith, to hold fast to our hope, and to stimulate one another to love. Faith, hope, and love. Faith and hope are evidenced by our love.

The HCSB translation says, "let us be concerned about one another," and the NLT says, "let us think of ways to motivate one another to acts of love and good works."

How do you show your concern and attention for fellow believers? How do you motivate them to acts of love? How have you been motivated?

The pastor is living out his message even as he writes it. This letter shows tremendous concern for believers, and he is making his points in order to motivate them to act faithfully toward the Lord.

What is one aspect of motivation, according to Hebrews 10:25? Let us encourage one another,

all the more, especially now _____.

What is wonderful about the Day that is approaching, according to 2 Thessalonians 2:1-2?

The Day of the Lord is coming. We don't know when, but it is definitely getting closer with every day that goes by!

Reflect on the insightful questions posed by Dr. Adolph Saphir (1831-1891), a Hungarian Jew who accepted Christ and became a minister and missionary. Note your responses to his questions below.[2]

- The second advent of our Lord is the most powerful, as well as the most constraining motive. Do we hope to be with Christ and all the saints in glory, and shall we not love the brethren, and minister unto them, while we are waiting together for His coming?

- Do we expect Christ to acknowledge us as His brethren, and shall we be ashamed of Christ's members, or treat them with cold neglect and indifference?

- Have we all to appear before the tribunal of Christ and to account for our stewardship, and shall we not be faithful and diligent in exercising whatever ministry is entrusted to us, as God hath bestowed unto each one of us His own measure and gift?

What happens in the Day of the Lord according to the following verses?

Isaiah 13:9

Isaiah 24:21-23

Isaiah 28:5

Joel 2:1-2

1 Thessalonians 5:2-3

It's intriguing and also perplexing to try to grasp all that the Lord has communicated about "the Day of the Lord." There are specific details given along with vague or mysterious aspects of that Day. I hope you were able to see that the Day of the Lord includes God's wrath on unbelievers and His blessings on His people.

Both aspects of the Day of the Lord are intended as motivation by the pastor writing the Hebrews. He has more to say about what is to come upon believers in the next few verses.

Read Hebrews 10:24-25 and Hebrews 3:12-14. Summarize the very important purposes of fellowship between believers.

*Do you think it's time to get your cookbooks out, stir up a casserole, and have a potluck fellowship? Does that give "**stir up** love and good works" a whole new meaning? Just make sure you talk about your faith, hope, love, and the Lord more than you talk about your recipes!*

When I hear how God is working in someone else's life, I am encouraged by their faith. Here are some conversation starters to help you engage in motivating one another to love and good works.

> *How can I pray for you?*
> *How has God been working in your life lately?*
> *What Scriptures are especially meaningful to you right now?*
> *Who is your favorite Bible character?*

Remember, we're on the same team. We need to cheer each other on. #HoldFasttoJesus #savedbygrace #childofGod

WARNING – WARNING – WARNING

LESSON 31: A Very Sober Warning — Repeated
Hebrews 10:26-39

Practice what you preach. Live out what you believe. Walk the talk. The pastor urged his friends to hold fast to the confession of their faith. And he told them what it would look like. And he warned them what would happen if they deliberately sinned against the Lord.

The passage we are about to study is a very challenging one. There are various perspectives on its meaning. But whatever interpretation you decide to accept, you will still see a very serious warning. Hebrews 10:26-31 is the same warning given in Hebrews 6:4-8, using different imagery.

I am thankful for the bold exhortation from the pastor because it is a continued emphasis on the undeniable, completed, eternal work of our Great High Priest Jesus Christ. He is the way—the only way. He is the truth—the only truth. He is the life—the only life.

Please pray that the Holy Spirit will confirm your understanding of your great salvation.

Please read Hebrews 10:26-39.

The passage you just read sheds much light on the situation of the Hebrews who received this letter. The pastor urges them to look to the future judgment, remember their past behavior, and resolve to endure their present difficulties.

Let's consider the easier verses first!

Regarding the <u>past</u>, according to Hebrews 10:32-34:

What were they to recall?

What did they experience?

Who did they help?

Why did they endure their sufferings in the past?

How would you summarize this previous behavior of the Hebrews? How did they live as followers of Christ?

Are you willing to take the same type of actions they took? And be treated as they were treated? Think about it. Pray about it.

Regarding the <u>present</u>, according to Hebrews 10:35-39:

What is the clear instruction (verse 35)?

What did they need?

What is the result of the clear instruction (verses 35-37)?

Instead of "drawing back," what were they to do (verses 38-39)?

Is this exhortation given to believers or unbelievers?

We'll come back to this encouraging and very important set of verses later.

But for now, you've seen the perspective and heart of the pastor for his people. He had seen their faith in action during past times of suffering and difficulty and harassment. His ultimate goal was for them to hold fast to their High Priest and endure their present hardships.

Commentators say that some of the recipients of the letter were Jews who had become Christians, but were considering going back to the Temple and the Levitical system of worship to avoid persecution as Christians.

So the pastor warned his people as seriously as he could.

As we study Hebrews 10:26-31 below, keep these two previous statements in mind: "let us draw near" (Hebrews 10:22), and "not forsaking the assembling of ourselves together as is the manner of some" (Hebrews 10:25).

Neglect of Christian fellowship is a symptom of imminent danger.

Look at the parallels to the previous warning in Hebrews 6. Write the phrases from Hebrews 10:26-31 that match the phrases given in Hebrews 6:4-8.

Hebrews 6:4-8	Hebrews 10:26-31
	10:26 Deliberately _____
	10:29 Trample _____
	10:29 Treat _____
6:4-5 Once for all brought into the light Have experienced the gift from heaven Have received a share in the Holy Spirit Have experienced the goodness of God's Word and the coming age	10:26 Have received _____ 10:29 Sanctified by _____
6:4, 6 It is impossible…to restore them to repentance	10:26 No longer _____
6:6, 8 Loss, curse, burning	10:27 Terrifying _____ Raging _____ 10:29 Severer _____ 10:31 It is a fearful thing _____

This warning is not hypothetical; rather, it is based on the biblical history of the Israelites.

Under Mosaic law, what was the difference in handling unintentional sin versus deliberate sin, according to the following verses?

Exodus 21:12-14

Numbers 15:27-31

Now let's remember the description of the defiant sin of the Israelites, which the pastor has highlighted in his letter as the example of what not to do.

Summarize Numbers 14:40-44 and Deuteronomy 1:43.

"For if we sin willfully after we have received the knowledge of the truth, there no longer remains a sacrifice for sins" (Hebrews 10:26). This verse must be understood in light of the Mosaic law. If the Christians reading this letter returned to the Temple and the Jewish form of worship and sacrifices, after knowing that all their sins were forgiven in Christ, they would be returning to a religion that had no capacity to forgive their sins.

This is one of the points the pastor has been making in his letter. The Mosaic law, the Old Covenant, could not and did not take away sins. It was symbolic for that time until Christ came as the perfect High Priest and perfect sacrifice.

For review, please note the truths from Hebrews 9:7-11.

So, what is the warning for us today in Hebrews 10:26-31? The behavior has been clearly addressed: don't forsake Christian fellowship. Hold fast the confession of our hope. We can even recognize a warning against blending Christianity with some other belief system. That's called syncretism. It is terribly dangerous and shows a lack of understanding of Christ's work and our salvation. People of religions all around the world have syncretized them throughout history. It's like they are trying to cover all the bases. But Jesus' blood covers all our sins!

Again, what's the warning for us? Don't forsake Christ or Christian fellowship. If we do, we will be subject to the discipline of God. The pastor will discuss this topic further in Hebrews 12.

Highlight the extreme words of **warning** in the chart on the previous page.

Judgment, punishment, and the vengeance of the Lord are definitely described as the consequence for the deliberate sin of drawing back from Christ. The sin described is willful; it is ongoing; it is habitual; it is a way of life rather than a sin of weakness or ignorance.

The pastor has been warning his readers since Chapter 2.

NAS **Hebrews 2:2-3** For if the word spoken through angels proved unalterable, and every transgression and disobedience received a just recompense, ³how shall we escape if we neglect so great a salvation?

The following words are used in Hebrews 10:27 and 29:

> **Judgment: Strong's #2920, Greek word: Krisis -** (1) as the action of a judge *decision, judgment* (Jn. 5:30); especially as the activity of God in a final time for judging *day of judgment* (Mt. 10:15); in an unfavorable sense *condemnation, punishment* (Rev. 18:10); (2) as a personal evaluation of someone else's actions *judgment* (Jn. 7:24); (3) as the standard by which judgments and evaluations are to be made *right, justice* (Mt. 12:18); (4) as the basis on which a judgment is made *reason for a judgment* (Jn. 3:19)[1]
>
> **Raging fire: Strong's #2205: Zelos and Strong's #4442: Pur -** literally, "zeal of fire." Fire is personified: glow or ardor of fire, that is, of Him who is "a consuming fire."[2]
>
> **Punishment: Strong's #5098, Greek word: Timōria -** *vindication*, that is, (by implication) a *penalty:* punishment.[3] Found only here in the New Testament, but its verbal form is used twice of physical penalty only (Acts 22:5; 26:11).[4] What is the exact nature of this punishment? Views differ. Some see it as the judgment of lake of fire for apostates. Others view it as severe chastisement at the hand of God in this life attended by the loss of reward at the judgment seat of Christ.[5]

I understand the exhortation of Hebrews 10:26-31 to have a parallel interpretation to that of Hebrews 6:4-8. You can look back at Option #6, pages 86-88 to see a summary of the previous warning.

How is God's punishment upon believers described in the following verses?

Acts 5:1-11

1 Corinthians 3:13-15

1 Corinthians 11:27-32

Are you hearing the loud clear warning? If you—a true believer filled with the Holy Spirit—deliberately sin, and remain in a lifestyle of sin, then God will decide how to punish you. This is also called the discipline of the Lord, as He takes action to correct and train us.

This is truly a sobering warning. What is your reaction?

I don't want to get in trouble. The fear of punishment from my parents, teachers, and the court system has always made me attentive to doing what is right.

While I have no fear of God's eternal wrath, as a result of the truths in Hebrews, I have a tremendous awareness of the potential for God's discipline if I deliberately and defiantly remain in sin.

I'm thankful for God's justice. He is worthy of obedience and honor.

My life—and yours—are saved by the once and for all time sacrifice of Jesus. No one and no thing is better.

Let us hold fast to Jesus.

> My hope is built on nothing less
> Than Jesus' blood and righteousness.
> I dare not trust the sweetest frame…
> But wholly lean on Jesus' name.
>
> When darkness veils His lovely face,
> I rest on His unchanging grace;
> In every high and stormy gale,
> My anchor holds within the veil.[6]

LESSON 32: Now Faith
Hebrews 11: 1-3

Now is the time for faith! This is the message of the pastor in the affirmative. We've seen his warnings: Don't neglect your great salvation. Don't doubt the word of God. Don't neglect your gathering together. Now he very clearly says what to do instead. Walk by faith. He has been emphasizing this throughout his entire letter.

Please pray that you will heed the urging of the Holy Spirit to trust and hope in the faithfulness of God.

*Let's connect the dots between the chapter divisions. Read Hebrews 10:35–11:3 below and highlight the words **confidence, faith** and **conviction**.*

NAS **Hebrews 10:35 - 11:3** Therefore, do not throw away your confidence, which has a great reward. ³⁶For you have need of endurance, so that when you have done the will of God, you may receive what was promised. ³⁷For yet in a very little while, He who is coming will come, and will not delay. ³⁸But My righteous one shall live by faith; And if he shrinks back, My soul has no pleasure in him. ³⁹But we are not of those who shrink back to destruction, but of those who have faith to the preserving of the soul. **Hebrews 11:1** Now faith is the assurance of things hoped for, the conviction of things not seen. ²For by it the men of old gained approval. ³By faith we understand that the worlds were prepared by the word of God, so that what is seen was not made out of things which are visible.

We can see, from the context of this passage, several important stipulations that are tied to our faith. What are they? What goes hand in hand with faith?

What are the outcomes of our faith, based on the passage above?

As I mentioned at the beginning of this lesson, the pastor has been emphasizing throughout his letter that Christians are to live by faith. Directing us to hold fast to Jesus by faith has been a crucial idea from the pastor. He has motivated us to hold fast to Jesus by warning us and by explaining the superiority of Jesus Christ.

At this point, the pastor will urge us to walk by faith because of the promises that are in store for us. He has given us the example of the unbelief of the Israelites as what not to do. In comparison, he gives us the example of many who have endured suffering and walked by faith. Here's a brief overview of the pastor's emphasis on faith:

- Moses was faithful as a servant. (Hebrews 3:5)
- Jesus was more faithful as a Son. (Hebrews 3:1-6)
- Unfaithful Israelites in the wilderness were not allowed to enter the Promised Land. (Hebrews 3:7-19)
- We are to imitate those who through faith and patience inherit the promises. (Hebrews 6:12)
- God is faithful to His promises. (Hebrews 6:13-20)
- We are to draw near to God in full assurance of faith in the completed work of Christ our High Priest. (Hebrews 10:19-22)
- God is faithful to His promises. (Hebrews 10:23)
- The righteous live by faith. (Hebrews 10:38)
- We are to be motivated by examples of faithful people throughout history. (Hebrews 11:1-40)
- Jesus is the source and perfecter of our faith who endured suffering for the joy set before Him. (Hebrews 12:2)

In the examples above, who is the **most** faithful?

According to Hebrews 10:36-37, what is the promise that we are waiting to see fulfilled?

The pastor quoted from Habakkuk 2:3-4:

ᴱˢⱽ **Habakkuk 2:3-4** For still the vision awaits its appointed time; it hastens to the end - it will not lie. If it seems slow, wait for it; it will surely come; it will not delay. ⁴ . . . the righteous shall live by his faith.

> The prophet Habakkuk cried out to God because of the oppression which was rife on every hand, and wondered when divine righteousness would at last be vindicated on earth. God answered his complaint and bade him be patient.[1]

The pastor quoted from the Septuagint which interpreted this passage as a Messianic prophecy of Christ's return:

ᴱˢⱽ **Hebrews 10:37** For yet in a very little while, He who is coming will come, and will not delay.

The pastor knew the oppression, difficulties, trials, and sufferings of the Hebrews to whom he was writing. He urged them to remember God's promise made through Habakkuk. Wait for the One who is coming! The righteous live by faith.

What circumstances are you experiencing? What and who are you waiting for? Are you waiting as the pastor urged us to in Hebrews 10:35-39?

Now faith! This might be a new motto for me. Because it reminds me that I need faith right now. And it reminds me of the rest of the beautiful, precious truth that the pastor gives us in Hebrews 11:1.

Please write Hebrews 11:1. Meditate on it. Memorize it.

Please look up the following words:
Faith: Strong's #4102
Greek word:
Greek definition:

Substance: Strong's #5287
Greek word:
Greek definition:

Evidence: Strong's #1650
Greek word:
Greek definition:

Based on the truth of Hebrews 11:1, and the definition of the words above, do you think that **faith** would be recognized in court as proof which would convince a judge and jury of the facts of the case?

Even if you answered "no" to the question above, the more important question is whether or not you recognize faith as proof.

Consider the statements below and note your reactions to them. Do you agree? Disagree? Do you have faith as it is described here?

- Things which in themselves have no existence as yet [but are promised by God] become real and substantial by the exercise of faith.[2]

- Physical eyesight produces conviction or evidence of visible things; faith is the organ which enables people to see the invisible order.[3]

- Faith does not bestow reality on things which have no substance or reality in themselves.[4]

- Biblical faith is not: wishful thinking; emotional fantasy; blind optimism; a "hope-so" feeling;[5] intellectual assent to doctrine; superstition; belief in spite of evidence.[6]

What are the real, invisible things that you have faith in?

Look at Hebrews 10:38 and Hebrews 11:1. Please merge these two verses. Keep in mind that the pastor was exhorting his readers to faith in action, rather than teaching a theoretical belief.

> We probably understand this statement best [Hebrews 11:1], if we remember that "faith" refers to a way of life. Thus, one might paraphrase, "Faith is living in accord with the reality of things hoped for," or "faith is living as if the things hoped for are real."[7]

With this study on faith as the foundation, we are ready to study the delightful and motivating walk through the history of faithful people of God!

I think it's easy to overlook the short statement in Hebrews 11:2. Why is faith so important, based on this verse?

I asked you to write out Hebrews 11:1 earlier and meditate on it, and memorize it if you don't already know it. I think I'll add Hebrews 11:2! That one short summary verse of the heroes of the faith encourages me to live by faith as they did. And the outcome will be the approval of God. I can imagine Him smiling at us, even now.

***Now** is the time for faith.*

LESSON 33: ENTERING THE HALL OF FAITH
Hebrews 11: 1-40

We don't know if the book of Hebrews was written at a desk or transcribed as a sermon was given. It is often called a written sermon. If this were a spoken sermon, I think that this section would have been a fascinating, fast-moving, jaw-dropping reminder of those who lived by faith. And the pastor uses the Old Testament to preach faith, not law. The whole Bible teaches us that salvation is by grace through faith, not works.

Please pray that the Holy Spirit will strengthen your faith.

Let's read all the way through Hebrews 11:1-40. Enjoy the journey through history without stopping. We'll back up and slow down after taking it all in.

Highlight each mention of "**by faith _____**" with the name of the individual or group. Make sure to highlight those referred to in verses 32-40, even when only pronouns are used.

^{NKJ} **Hebrews 11:1-40** Now faith is the substance of things hoped for, the evidence of things not seen. ²For by it the elders obtained a good testimony. ³By faith we understand that the worlds were framed by the word of God, so that the things which are seen were not made of things which are visible. ⁴By faith Abel offered to God a more excellent sacrifice than Cain, through which he obtained witness that he was righteous, God testifying of his gifts; and through it he being dead still speaks. ⁵By faith Enoch was taken away so that he did not see death, "and was not found, because God had taken him;" for before he was taken he had this testimony, that he pleased God. ⁶But without faith it is impossible to please Him, for he who comes to God must believe that He is, and that He is a rewarder of those who diligently seek Him. ⁷By faith Noah, being divinely warned of things not yet seen, moved with godly fear, prepared an ark for the saving of his household, by which he condemned the world and became heir of the righteousness which is according to faith. ⁸By faith Abraham obeyed when he was called to go out to the place which he would receive as an inheritance. And he went out, not knowing where he was going. ⁹By faith he dwelt in the land of promise as in a foreign country, dwelling in tents with Isaac and Jacob, the heirs with him of the same promise; ¹⁰for he waited for the city which has foundations, whose builder and maker is God. ¹¹By faith Sarah herself also received strength to conceive seed, and she bore a child when she was past the age, because

she judged Him faithful who had promised. [12]Therefore from one man, and him as good as dead, were born as many as the stars of the sky in multitude -- innumerable as the sand which is by the seashore. [13]These all died in faith, not having received the promises, but having seen them afar off were assured of them, embraced them and confessed that they were strangers and pilgrims on the earth. [14]For those who say such things declare plainly that they seek a homeland. [15]And truly if they had called to mind that country from which they had come out, they would have had opportunity to return. [16]But now they desire a better, that is, a heavenly country. Therefore God is not ashamed to be called their God, for He has prepared a city for them. [17]By faith Abraham, when he was tested, offered up Isaac, and he who had received the promises offered up his only begotten son, [18]of whom it was said, "In Isaac your seed shall be called," [19]concluding that God was able to raise him up, even from the dead, from which he also received him in a figurative sense. [20]By faith Isaac blessed Jacob and Esau concerning things to come. [21]By faith Jacob, when he was dying, blessed each of the sons of Joseph, and worshiped, leaning on the top of his staff. [22]By faith Joseph, when he was dying, made mention of the departure of the children of Israel, and gave instructions concerning his bones. [23]By faith Moses, when he was born, was hidden three months by his parents, because they saw he was a beautiful child; and they were not afraid of the king's command. [24]By faith Moses, when he became of age, refused to be called the son of Pharaoh's daughter, [25]choosing rather to suffer affliction with the people of God than to enjoy the passing pleasures of sin, [26]esteeming the reproach of Christ greater riches than the treasures in Egypt; for he looked to the reward. [27]By faith he forsook Egypt, not fearing the wrath of the king; for he endured as seeing Him who is invisible. [28]By faith he kept the Passover and the sprinkling of blood, lest he who destroyed the firstborn should touch them. [29]By faith they passed through the Red Sea as by dry land, whereas the Egyptians, attempting to do so, were drowned. [30]By faith the walls of Jericho fell down after they were encircled for seven days. [31]By faith the harlot Rahab did not perish with those who did not believe, when she had received the spies with peace. [32]And what more shall I say? For the time would fail me to tell of Gideon and Barak and Samson and Jephthah, also of David and Samuel and the prophets: [33]who through faith subdued kingdoms, worked righteousness, obtained promises, stopped the mouths of lions, [34]quenched the violence of fire, escaped the edge of the sword, out of weakness were made strong, became valiant in battle, turned to flight the armies of the aliens. [35]Women received their dead raised to life again. And others were tortured, not accepting deliverance, that they might obtain a better resurrection.

³⁶Still others had trial of mockings and scourgings, yes, and of chains and imprisonment. ³⁷They were stoned, they were sawn in two, were tempted, were slain with the sword. They wandered about in sheepskins and goatskins, being destitute, afflicted, tormented— ³⁸of whom the world was not worthy. They wandered in deserts and mountains, in dens and caves of the earth. ³⁹And all these, having obtained a good testimony through faith, did not receive the promise, ⁴⁰God having provided something better for us, that they should not be made perfect apart from us.

What is your initial reaction to this chapter? Is it inspiring? Challenging? Do you want to know the people? Would you behave as they did? Do you want to?

To get the big idea that the pastor wanted to communicate from this section, we need to read through it again. This time **highlight with different colors** than you used for "by faith": **Color #1:** any words or phrases which describe **suffering, trials, hardship; Color #2:** any words or phrases that refer **to the promises of God and His rewards.**

Reflect on what you have highlighted, and read Hebrews 10:35-39, then summarize the big idea that the pastor is communicating through Hebrews 11.

There is one more survey of Hebrews 11 that I would like you to see. The thesis of this particular passage is in verse 1, and the rest of the chapter supports that thesis.

Because repetition is an excellent teacher, (and because I challenged you to memorize this verse!), please write out Hebrews 11:1.

It's very obvious that the key word is faith which is repeated throughout chapter 11. The concept expressed in verse 1 is also referred to several times in the chapter.

Note the truths in the following verses that correspond to the thesis statement above.

Hebrews 11:3 By faith we _____

       Things which are seen were _____

Hebrews 11:7 By faith Noah, when warned about things _____

Hebrews 11:13 Not having received the promises, but _____

Hebrews 11:26 By faith Moses…looked to the _____

Hebrews 11:27 He (Moses) endured _____

Summarize what these statements emphasize about faith.

Because the recipients of this letter were struggling in their circumstances and in their faith, and because they were well-acquainted with their Jewish heritage, the pastor reminds them of the circumstances and faith of the most well-known people of God.

What does Hebrews 6:12 tell us to do?

The readers of this letter were not hearing about these heroes for the first time. Let's look at what the rest of Scripture tells us about Abel, Enoch, and Noah. Commentators refer to them as the "antediluvians," which means they lived before the flood. And of course, Noah lived through it!

The Faith of Abel:

Read Genesis 4:3-5. What did Abel do and what was God's response?

Read Genesis 4:6-7. What did God require of Cain?

Read Genesis 4:8-10. What did Cain do and what is said about Abel?

Read Matthew 23:35. How did Jesus refer to Abel?

Read 1 John 3:12. How is Abel's action described?

> Since Cain was told that he would be accepted if he did well (Genesis 4:7), it follows that Abel was accepted because he did well—because, in other words, he was righteous. And in fact the righteousness of Abel is emphasized elsewhere in the New Testament.[1]

The pastor made his statement about Abel based on the words of Genesis and the words of Jesus. He concluded that because God approved of Abel's offering, Abel had presented them in righteousness by faith.

> But how could it be known that it was "by faith" that Abel brought God a more acceptable sacrifice than his brother? Probably the close association between righteousness and faith in Hebrews 10:38, "my righteous one will live by faith," was ground sufficient in our author's eyes for his statement about Abel's faith. And the affirmation in Hebrews 11:6 is applicable to Abel: "without faith it is impossible to please God" —and since Abel manifestly pleased Him, it follows that Abel lived and acted by faith.[2]

Read Hebrews 11:4. How can you imitate Abel's faith?

The Faith of Enoch:

Read Genesis 5:18-27. How old was Enoch's father Jared when he died?

What did Enoch do after he fathered Methuselah?

What happened when Enoch was 365 years old?

How old was Enoch's son Methuselah when he died?

Based on the verses above and Hebrews 11:5-6, what is emphasized about Enoch that is the example for us?

To walk humbly with our God is His fundamental requirement. The prophet Micah said: "The Lord has told you what is good, and this is what He requires of you: to do what is right, to love mercy, and to walk humbly with your God." Micah 6:8 ^{NLT}

How can you imitate the faith of Enoch?

The Faith of Noah:

Read Genesis 6:5-12. What were the circumstances?

How was Noah different from the rest of the people?

Read Genesis 6:13-22. What did God say would happen?

What was Noah to do and what did he do?

Read Ezekiel 14:14. How is Noah described here?

Read 2 Peter 2:5. How is Noah described here?

Read Hebrews 11:7. What 3 actions or attitudes demonstrated Noah's faith?

The first is implied: He believed God's warning.

The second was a heart response: _____

The third was visible action: _____

> What is emphasized here is that when God announced that He would do something unprecedented in the experience of Noah and his contemporaries, Noah took Him at His word, and showed that he did so by making practical preparations against the day when that word would come true. Noah received a divine communication that a deluge would sweep over the earth. Such a catastrophe had never been known before, but Noah's faith supplied the proof of "things not seen." [3]

Because the pastor has been warning the Hebrews to live by faith, be patient and endure suffering, and anticipate the promises of God, Noah is an excellent example. He responded to God's warning. He patiently endured about 100 years of building the ark when no one had ever experienced flood (and maybe not even a rainstorm). Those around him perished because they did not heed the warning preached by Noah. And he became "an heir of the righteousness which comes by faith" (Hebrews 11:7).

How can you imitate the faith of Noah?

We've entered the Hall of Faith. We've looked around and have seen the magnificent mural painted by the pastor. We've seen real faith by real people who knew our real God.

You know there is much more to see. There are more examples to imitate.

May we be faithful, as they were, so that we too may become examples to those who come after us.

> Oh may all who come behind us find us faithful
> May the fire of our devotion light their way
> May the footprints that we leave
> Lead them to believe
> And the lives we live inspire them to obey
> Oh may all who come behind us find us faithful. [4]

LESSON 34: FATHER ABRAHAM AND THE FAITHFUL PATRIARCHS
HEBREWS 11: 8-22

How well do you know Abraham, Isaac, Jacob, and Joseph? Perhaps you know quite a bit about the events of their lives. The book of Genesis gives us interesting narratives about their travels, their marriages, their challenges, and God's blessings on them.

The pastor highlights a few aspects of their experiences which show us that they lived by faith even when the promises of God remained in the distant future instead of their immediate present. The pastor wants his readers to follow their example.

Please pray that the Holy Spirit will lead you to walk by faith as God's people did long ago.

Let's see what the pastor points out about Abraham. He was first mentioned in Genesis 11:26 as Abram, the son of Terah, who lived in Ur of the Chaldeans. Then his life is detailed from Genesis 12-25. He is referred to repeatedly throughout the whole Bible, about 230 times. He is referred to 10 times in the book of Hebrews. And Jesus often mentioned him.

What were Abraham's behaviors that demonstrated his faith in God, according to the following verses?

Hebrews 11:8

Hebrews 11:9

Hebrews 11:10

Hebrews 11:17

On what promises of God were all of Abraham's actions based? See Genesis 12:1-4.

One of the things that we have seen in the letter to the Hebrews is the emphasis on the Word of God. "In the past, God spoke." We are to pay attention to, believe, and obey the Word of God.

> The pastor emphasizes the immediacy of Abraham's response. In Greek, the initial "by faith" is followed immediately by the present participle "being called" and the aorist verb "he obeyed." This construction is appropriately translated, "as soon as Abraham was called he obeyed." There was no hesitation or procrastination. What a contrast with the people of the wilderness generation, who repeatedly expressed their unbelief through disobedience.[1]

*Abraham faced similar circumstances to those that every believer has faced. God has made promises to us that we are waiting to see fulfilled. The way things **seem to be right now** is not the final story. There is **reality** in the promises of God. Abraham's example prompts us to obey and have faith in God's Word even when we don't see the evidence of its fulfillment in our present situation.*

How did things **seem to be** for Abraham, compared to the **reality of God's promise**? Look at Hebrews 11:8-12? (Include the example of Sarah's faith as well.)

> By faith Sarah experienced the real but unseen power of God in the present through the birth of Isaac.[2]

The pastor inserts an important commentary on the faith of Abraham, Sarah, Isaac, and Jacob at Hebrews 11:13-16. He says "these all died in faith." He emphasizes that the way things seemed to be did not deter them from faith.

How are the fathers described in Hebrews 11:13-14? Try to list 6 points.

1.

2.

3.

4.

5.

6.

What contrast is given in Hebrews 11:15-16?

Keep in mind that the pastor has been urging his readers not to draw back from Jesus, and not to neglect the assembly of believers.

> The place God had promised Abraham was ultimately not the earthly land of Canaan but a City that has foundations, whose architect and builder is God. This City is the future hoped for object of his people's faith.[3]

Keep in mind also that the pastor has taught that the earthly tabernacle is only a shadow of the heavenly tabernacle. We are promised and waiting for the heavenly city, the heavenly country, and the heavenly tabernacle.

If the things we see and experience on earth are just temporary, what should our attitude toward things of earth be?

It's time to consider death and dying. It's very important to include this topic in the discussion about faith.

Please read Genesis 22:1-14.

How do Genesis 22:1 and Hebrews 11:17 explain the command of God?

The words "offered" and "offering" are used in both Genesis and Hebrews. What would have happened to Isaac if God had not stopped Abraham from offering him on the altar?

What did Abraham say about himself and Isaac in Genesis 22:5?

What was God's evaluation of Abraham, according to Genesis 22:12?

What did Abraham have faith in, according to Hebrews 11:19?

Oh, we are observing a watershed moment in Abraham's life! Trusting that God can raise someone from the dead is so, so important. This is a big deal! Believing in Jesus' resurrection from the dead makes a difference in your eternity.

Please note what Paul said regarding resurrection from the dead in 1 Corinthians 15:12-14.

What is the good news and good hope for us, according to 1 Corinthians 15:20-23?

Christ is risen! He is risen indeed! And because He was raised from the dead, I know that I too will be raised from the dead.

Faith in the resurrection is actually a central theme to Hebrews 11. Keep your eyes open for references to God's power over death and indications that the heroes of faith were looking ahead to their life after death. We've already noticed that Abraham, Isaac, and Jacob longed for the heavenly country.

The pastor reminded the Hebrews of the dying declarations of their faithful fathers. Highlighting these words shows that they were looking to the future in which God would keep His promises.

How was faith demonstrated by Isaac, Jacob, and Joseph, according to Hebrews 11:20-22? Optional: See also Genesis 28:1-4; 48:15-16; 49:1, 28.

> The faith of Joseph was certainly remarkable. After the way his family treated him, you would think he would have abandoned his faith, but instead, it grew stronger. Even ungodly influence of Egypt did not weaken his trust in God. Joseph did not use his family, his job, or his circumstances as an excuse for unbelief. [4]

I am fascinated by the faith of Joseph. He never knew his great-great-grandfather Abraham but he knew what God had said to him. And Joseph believed God.

What specifically did Joseph anticipate, that God said to Abraham, according to Genesis 15:13-21 and Genesis 50:24-26?

> Joseph gives this command because he wants to go continue his identity with the people of God even after his death. He will go with them and inherit the future that God has for them—including the resurrection of his bones.
>
> The pastor would have his hearers remember God's promises, believe that His promises transcend death, and persist in their identity with the people of God so that they might enter into the final inheritance promised by God. [5]

Why was Joseph a powerful example of faith for the Hebrews to whom this letter was written?

Review **the faith of Abraham** in Hebrews 11:8-19. How can you imitate his faith in God?

Review **the faith of Isaac, Jacob, and Joseph** in Hebrews 11:20-22. How can you imitate their faith in the promises of God?

LESSON 35: MOSES AND MORE FAITHFUL FOLLOWERS OF GOD
HEBREWS 11: 23-31

"Let my people go!" This is what the Lord told Moses to go tell the Pharaoh of Egypt. Was his obedience to this command the defining moment of Moses' faith? It was part of it. But it's not the behavior that's highlighted in Hebrews 11. We will see that difficult circumstances in Moses' life didn't hinder his faith. It's his endurance that is the example that the pastor wants his people to follow.

Please pray that you will obey the Holy Spirit and walk by faith in every circumstance.

The Lord's people—the Israelites—were slaves in Egypt. In the last lesson, we saw that the Lord had promised Abraham, Isaac, and Jacob that their descendants would be enslaved and oppressed in a foreign country for 400 years. It is fascinating to me that the Lord gave Abraham this information in advance. It's really bad news. But the good news was that the oppression of Egypt would come to an end.

Some Israelites kept this truth in their hearts and in their prayers.

What did the Lord tell Moses in Exodus 3:7-9?

That's the big picture of the difficult circumstances into which Moses was born. Let's look at the specific terrible law of the land at his birth.

What did the Pharaoh of Egypt decree, according to Exodus 1:15-16 and Exodus 1:22?

Imagine what it would have been like for pregnant Hebrew women and their husbands at that time. Grief. Fear. Agony. We know that the Hebrew midwives Shiphrah and Puah were courageous and saved the lives of many baby boys (Exodus 1:17-21). We don't know if they helped Moses' parents, Amram and Jochebed (Exodus 6:20). But we do know that his parents lived by faith during this distressing time.

The Faith of Moses' Parents:

Read Hebrews 11:23 and note what Amram and Jochebed did—by faith. List 3 actions.

What is your reaction to their faith?

What might be a modern-day action that would be similar to their faith?

Oh, what a beautiful baby! That's a common reaction to seeing a little one, isn't it? But when Amram and Jochebed saw their baby boy, something about him prompted great faith. The word "beautiful" in the Hebrew language (Exodus 2:2) is "tov" and basically means good, in every possible meaning. Pleasing. Desirable. Useable. Suitable. Good in character. Acts 7:20 tells us that Moses was beautiful in God's sight. Commentators think that this means that Moses was more than just a beautiful baby. That he was no ordinary child, as the NIV translates it. That Moses' parents realized that God would use him.

*Moses' parents had faith to **see** that which was hoped for, to **see** that which was unseen. And they were not afraid.*

The Faith of Moses:

Read Hebrews 11:24-28 and note what Moses did—by faith. List 8 actions.

The summary of Moses' faith is very brief when you consider that the books of Exodus, Leviticus, Numbers, and Deuteronomy tell us about the faithful leadership of Moses. Does it surprise you that big events such as the plagues and the receiving of the Ten Commandments weren't mentioned?

What type of circumstances and acts of faith are highlighted in Hebrews 11:24-28? Remember how the pastor has been exhorting his readers. What is it about Moses that the pastor wants his people to imitate?

Let's make sure we notice that Moses identified "with the people of God." He was one of them but had been raised in the Pharaoh's household. He left the lifestyle of the rich and famous and returned to his people even though they were suffering.

What specifically is to be the reason for enduring affliction, according to Hebrews 11:26?

> The vast value of the treasures of Egypt was legendary, yet Moses refused to compare Egypt's treasures with God's promised reward.[1]

> We have already seen that through the divine revelation Moses received as steward in God's house he was a witness to the things that would be said by God in Christ (Hebrews 1:1; 3:5). Thus, there is no need to assume that the pastor thinks Moses received some special vision apart from Scripture. Moses knew that by his sufferings he identified with the Christ who was to come.[2]

What did Jesus tell his disciples about suffering for the name of Christ? See Matthew 5:10-12.

Blessed. And rewarded. Possibly on earth, but definitely in heaven. We must keep looking ahead.

It's life after death that we are looking ahead to. In the previous lesson, we observed that faith in God's power to raise the dead is a recurring theme throughout this chapter. While there isn't a specific statement regarding death and resurrection in the example of faith in Moses' life, there are circumstances that allude to it. Baby Moses was saved from death; Moses survived the wrath of the king who wanted to kill him (Exodus 2:15); the Passover and blood on the doorposts saved Israelites from the death of their firstborn. (Exodus 12:12-13)

Read Hebrews 11:23-28 once more. How can you imitate the faith of Moses and his parents?

Who are the next three examples of faith in Hebrews 11:29-31? These provide the sequel to Moses' life.

You don't need to turn back to the original record of these events to grasp the details of what happened. But these events, although well-known to God's people, were still mysterious! How did God divide the sea, push back the waves, and make the sand dry—for more than 2 million people to walk through the walls of water? How did marching around Jericho for 7 days make the walls of the city fall down? How did Rahab's house of harlotry in the wall of Jericho become the safe place for the Israelite spies and why did God save her?

*Archeology and history try to give us answers to these questions, but "the forces which operate in the unseen realm, such as the power of faith, cannot be dug up by the excavator's spade." *[3]

If you do want more details about these big events, you can find them here: the parting of the Red Sea – Exodus 14:9-31; the fall of Jericho – Joshua 6:1-21; the saving of Rahab – Joshua 6:22-25.

According to Hebrews 11:29-31, who **lived** in these three examples, and why? Who **died,** and why?

It's no surprise to say that the pastor wants his people to focus on the faith of the people of God. In these examples, the emphasis is on having faith in God's real, yet unseen, power in the present. The previous examples emphasized a faith that looked toward future rewards. We have to have that. But these examples show us the faith of those who trusted God's power to deliver them at the height of a desperate crisis.

We have to have faith in God to see us through our circumstances today.

How is your faith? Do you only trust God for your future, and not your troubles today? Do you have trouble trusting God for your future because of your difficulties today?

Please end the lesson with praise to our God who is faithful to His word and faithful to His people. Great is His faithfulness every day in every way.

NAS Psalm 146:1-2, 5-10

Praise the LORD! Praise the LORD, O my soul! ²I will praise the LORD while I live; I will sing praises to my God while I have my being. How blessed is he whose help is the God of Jacob, Whose hope is in the LORD his God; ⁶Who made heaven and earth, The sea and all that is in them; Who keeps faith forever; ⁷Who executes justice for the oppressed; Who gives food to the hungry. The LORD sets the prisoners free. ⁸The LORD opens the eyes of the blind; The LORD raises up those who are bowed down; The LORD loves the righteous; ⁹The LORD protects the strangers; He supports the fatherless and the widow; But He thwarts the way of the wicked. ¹⁰The LORD will reign forever, Thy God, O Zion, to all generations. Praise the LORD!

LESSON 36: UNLIKELY HEROES OF THE FAITH
HEBREWS 11:32

Surprise! Guess what? You wouldn't think the next four men in Hebrews 11:32 would be examples to imitate! And maybe that's the point! God is faithful to each person who is faithful to Him, no matter how weak or unwise they may be. None of us have an excuse to not trust God. He's not just good to the wise and noble, but to every person that looks to Him through Christ for their strength and salvation.

Please pray that the Holy Spirit will convict you of any unbelief and convince you to be strong in faith in the Lord.

Please read Hebrews 11:32.

Why were the first 4 men named as heroes of the faith? Commentators point out that they do seem to be unusual candidates. However, these 4 men are named in 1 Samuel 12:11 as being sent by the Lord to deliver the Israelites out of the hands of their enemies; so the pastor is once again referencing Old Testament Scripture. Of Gideon, Jephthah, and Samson, it is said that the Spirit of the Lord came upon them.

The Faith of Gideon:

Read Judges 6:11-16. What was Gideon doing when the angel of the Lord appeared to him and why?

What was Gideon's assessment of himself?

How did the Lord say that Gideon would save Israel?

Gideon is a paradox, isn't he? A mighty warrior? Hiding in a winepress so that no one would see him or hear him threshing wheat. And the runt of the litter. Gideon meets the Lord and makes him dinner. The Lord consumes it—with fire! Gideon believes he has seen the Lord; he obeys His command; he calls tribes of Israel to fight with him against the Midianites. Then he has doubts about whether God will save Israel through him. The Lord assures him two days in a row.

Read Judges 7:2-7. Gideon's army began with 32,000 men. What did the Lord say about that?

> How did Gideon respond when the Lord commanded him to send men home?

Read Judges 7:8-18. How is the faith of Gideon displayed in this account?

Hail to the mighty warrior Gideon! Not because he was super strong or because he led a supersized army. But because his simple faith was stretched and grew strong!

How can you imitate the faith of Gideon?

The Faith of Barak:

Read Judges 4:1-7. Who oppressed Israel? And how large was his army?

> What was the message of the Lord to Barak?

Taking 10,000 men to fight against 900 iron chariots might sound like a numerical victory. The reality was that iron chariots had sharp blades projecting about 14 feet from both sides of the wheels. These could cut the enemy to pieces in battle. And the chariots carried multiple archers with a large arsenal of bows and arrows. The Israelites were paralyzed with fear.

It was this terrorizing Canaanite army that Barak was commanded by the Lord to defeat.

Read Judges 4:8-16. What did Barak do?

> Do you think that Barak acted courageously? Why or why not?

Read Judges 5:1-9. Who received credit for the victory against the Canaanites Jabin and Sisera?

How can you imitate the faith of Barak?

The Faith of Jephthah:

His name is strange and his story is stranger. But he is a man of faith. Let's see why.

Read Judges 11:1-11. How does Jephthah demonstrate his faith in his response to the call to fight the Ammonites?

Jephthah agreed to fight the Ammonites and his first move was to send their king a message: "What do you have against us that you have attacked our country?" The king replied (my paraphrase): because Israel took my land from me and I want it back. Jephthah's incredible response is recorded in Judges 11:15-24 and rehearses the Exodus, the wilderness wanderings, and the Israelites' conquest of territories based on the command of the Lord. His conclusion is: God took the land of Israel from the Amorites, not the Ammonites. The king should keep what his god (Chemosh) gives him and the Israelites will keep what their God gives them.

The king of the Ammonites didn't like that at all.

Read Judges 11:28-40. How is faith in the Lord demonstrated by Jephthah in verses 30-32?

How is Jephthah's faith demonstrated in verse 35?

Much to our surprise, Jephthah is a man of faith, who "in spite of his foolish, horrific vow, led in the defeat of the Amorites." [1]

> Posterity remembers him chiefly for his rash vow; yet, rash as it was, it was a token of his sincere though uninstructed devotion to the God of Israel.[2]

What perspective does Paul give us about the wise and foolish in 1 Corinthians 1:26-31?

How can you imitate the faith of Jephthah?

Are you ready for the next unlikely hero of faith? Jephthah made one rash vow. Samson made many wrong choices!

The Faith of Samson:

> It is not by any means necessary to suppose that in making mention of Samson, the [pastor] approved of all that he did. All that he commands is his faith, and though he was a very imperfect man, and there were many things in his life which neither sound morality nor religion can approve, yet it was still true that he evinced, on some occasions, remarkable confidence in God, by relying on the strength which he gave him. This was particularly true in the instance where he made a great slaughter of the enemies of the Lord, and of his country.[3]

Samson's story begins wonderfully in Judges 13:3 and ends tragically in Judges 16:31. In these three chapters, we learn of his strength, his desire for the wrong women, his wit, and his wrath.

Read Judges 15:14-20. What did Samson do?

To whom does Samson attribute his strength and success?

Read Judges 16:23-31. How does Samson demonstrate his faith here?

Samson was loyal to his people and to his God. He lived under the oppression of the Philistines and fought against them for the sake of Israel. When there was no other way to defeat them but to give up his life, he did so by faith. He prayed, and his prayer was heard by the Lord who accepted it and answered it. Samson's strength didn't come from natural ability or a Nazarite vow or long hair. His strength came from the Lord and his dependence on Him.

How can you imitate the faith of Samson?

The Faith of David:

And now—the kind of hero we all want. Or is he? King David is next in the list. Time definitely is too short to tell of all of his acts of faith and experiences of failure. Please observe a few important truths about David from the Scriptures.

What does 1 Samuel 16:12-13 tell us about David?

What does 1 Samuel 17:26 and 32-37 tell us about the faith of David?

What does Acts 13:22 tell us about David?

David expressed his faith in many ways, including poetry and song. What did he declare by faith in Psalm 145:1-6? You can read the whole psalm!

How can you imitate the faith of David?

The Faith of Samuel:

The list of named heroes ends with Samuel. His name also leads us into the next section of unnamed prophets and then the rest of the unnamed heroes. Rather than being an unlikely hero of faith, if there had been a "Most Likely to be Faithful" contest in the Old Testament, Samuel probably would have been selected. His mother Hannah prayed passionately for his birth. She dedicated him to the Lord. He grew up serving at the Tabernacle. He started obeying the voice of the Lord at a young age. As an adult, he served Israel as a judge and a priest.

How was the faith of Samuel demonstrated in 1 Samuel 7:3-16?

Samuel showed the Israelites that God was still in their midst and was powerful to save. He grieved when they rejected God as their King. He later had the privilege of anointing and encouraging David.

How can you imitate the faith of Samuel?

Consider the situations that Gideon, Barak, Jephthah, Samson, David, and Samuel faced. Each engaged in battles against very strong enemies. What did the faith of these men allow them to **see** that was unseen?

Think about the big message that the pastor has been emphasizing to the Hebrews. Even in hard times when circumstances seem to be all against you, trust in Jesus Christ who saves.

LESSON 37: UNNAMED HEROES OF THE FAITH
HEBREWS 11: 32-40

Surprise again! And shock and awe. The unnamed heroes—and heroines—of faith endured much adversity and affliction. The Lord knows your name and your faithful obedience to Him even when no one else does.

Remember that this is not just a moment of honorary recognition of these people of God. They are examples of those who lived by faith and did not shrink back from suffering for the Lord. This is the way the pastor urged the Hebrews to live when he quoted the Lord's words to Habakkuk:

^{NET} **Hebrews 10:38-39** But my righteous one will live by faith, and if he shrinks back, I take no pleasure in him. ³⁹But we are not among those who shrink back and thus perish, but are among those who have faith and preserve their souls.

Please pray that the Holy Spirit will empower you to draw near to the Lord and have enduring faith in Him through all circumstances.

Please read Hebrews 11:32-40.

List the details of these verses in the appropriate columns below. I've given you a few examples. There is no need to match the information from column to column. (Gideon wasn't tortured.)

Named and Unnamed Heroes	Miraculous Deliverances	Sufferings Endured
v.32 Gideon	v.33 subdued kingdoms	v.35 torture

This exercise is to help us see that all kinds of people lived by faith. All kinds of people experienced God's power and were rescued and victorious. And all kinds of people endured tremendous suffering and even death—by faith—because they knew that there is more to life than life on earth.

From memory, if possible, write out Hebrews 11:1. (Check your work against Scripture to make sure you get it right.)

Please write out Hebrews 11:6 as well.

How does the pastor indicate that the unnamed heroes of the faith pleased God, according to Hebrews 11:38-39?

Is God's approval always indicated by the removal of suffering? Explain your answer.

I am so thankful for the teachings and testimony of Paul, regarding tribulations. Note what you learn from the verses below.

Acts 14:22

Acts 20:22-24

Romans 5:3

2 Corinthians 6:4-5; 9-10

2 Thessalonians 1:3-5

Suffering comes in all shapes and sizes. Suffering comes into our lives for a variety of reasons. The book of Hebrews demonstrates that suffering can be a consequence of sin (Hebrews 3:17-19) and the pastor will explain this discipline of God further in Hebrews 12.

But here in Hebrews 11, the pastor emphasizes that even the righteous who live by faith may suffer terribly and not see God's rescue from affliction on earth.

Those who live by faith are waiting for what? Note what the verses below tell us.

Hebrews 11:10

Hebrews 11:13

Hebrews 11:14

Hebrews 11:16

Hebrews 11:26

Hebrews 11:35

The truths of Scripture that we've studied so far in this lesson give us the biblical worldview that we must not forget. Sometimes terribly painful trials and tribulations are allowed in our lives by God. The brief list of experiences of unnamed heroes of the faith shows us that people of God have persevered and endured awful sorrow, distress, and torture.

The pastor didn't name these incredible heroes of faith, but he was thinking of real people. He based his list on people in the Bible as well as people of God from history. I find it very encouraging to remember those who kept the faith under dreadful and excruciating conditions.

Those with access to the biblical record, as well as books of Jewish history, have suggested that the following people may have been the ones referred to in Hebrews 11:33-38. As you read this biblical history, consider who you would want to interview if you could talk to them right now.

By faith:

Prophets such as Elijah, Elisha, Amos, Hosea, Isaiah, and Jeremiah – spoke and acted for God

HCSB **1 Kings 18:21-24** ²¹ Then Elijah approached all the people and said, "How long will you hesitate between two opinions? If Yahweh is God, follow Him. But if Baal, follow him." But the people didn't answer him a word. ²² Then Elijah said to the people …. ²³ "Let two bulls be given to us. They are to choose one bull for themselves, cut it in pieces, and place it on the wood but not light the fire. I will prepare the other bull and place it on the wood but not light the fire. ²⁴ Then you call on the name of your god, and I will call on the name of Yahweh. The God who answers with fire, He is God." All the people answered, "That sounds good."

Joshua, the judges, and David - subdued kingdoms (Joshua 11:15-19; Judges 6:1-13:33; 2 Samuel 8:12)

NIV **Psalm 44:1-3** We have heard with our ears, O God; our fathers have told us what you did in their days, in days long ago. ²With your hand you drove out the nations and planted our fathers; you crushed the peoples and made our fathers flourish. ³It was not by their sword that they won the land, nor did their arm bring them victory; it was your right hand, your arm, and the light of your face, for you loved them.

David – established righteousness (2 Samuel 8:15)

NAS **2 Samuel 8:15** So David reigned over all Israel; and David administered justice and righteousness for all his people.

David and Solomon – obtained promises (2 Samuel 7:12-17; 1 Kings 5:5)

CSB **1 Kings 5:5** So I plan to build a temple for the name of the LORD my God, according to what the LORD promised my father David: "I will put your son on your throne in your place, and he will build the temple for My name."

Daniel – shut the mouths of lions (Daniel 6:1-8) "He was thrown into the lions' den for his fidelity to God, but protected from their attacks because, in his own words, "I was found blameless before Him." [1]

Shadrach, Meshach, and Abednego – quenched the power of fire (Daniel 3:1-30) They refused to bow down and worship Nebuchadnezzar's golden image; the penalty was death by fire. "Had they received a special revelation that their lives would be preserved, it would have called for considerable faith to act upon it in the face of the burning fiery furnace, but to behave as they did without any revelation of the kind called for much greater faith." [2]

Many, including Elijah, Elisha, and Jeremiah – escaped the edge of the sword (1 Samuel 18:11; 1 Kings 19:2-18; 2 Kings 6:31-7:2; Jeremiah 36:19, 26)

NIV **Jeremiah 26:16** Then the officials and all the people said to the priests and the prophets, "This man [Jeremiah] should not be sentenced to death! He has spoken to us in the name of the LORD our God."

Many judges, prophets, and kings – were made powerful out of weakness (Judges 6:15; 16:28), became strong in battle, and put foreign armies to flight (1 Samuel 14:6; 2 Chronicles 14:11-14; 2 Chronicles 32:20-22)

^{ESV} **2 Chronicles 14:11-12** And [King] Asa cried to the LORD his God, "O LORD, there is none like you to help, between the mighty and the weak. Help us, O LORD our God, for we rely on you, and in your name we have come against this multitude. O LORD, you are our God; let not man prevail against you." ¹²So the LORD defeated the Ethiopians before Asa and before Judah, and the Ethiopians fled.

The poor widow of Zarephath and the wealthy woman of Shunem – received their dead raised to life again (1 Kings 17:17-24; 2 Kings 4:17-37)

^{ESV} **1 Kings 17:23-24** And Elijah said, "See, your son lives." ²⁴And the woman said to Elijah, "Now I know that you are a man of God, and that the word of the LORD in your mouth is truth."

Others – were tortured to death refusing to accept deliverance

> The particular form of torture indicated by the Greek verb is being stretched on a frame and beaten to death. The was precisely the punishment meted out to Eleazar, one of the noble confessors of the Maccabaean days, who willingly accepted death rather than forswear his loyalty to God. In 2 Maccabees the story of his martyrdom is followed by the record of the mother and her seven sons who endured this and other forms of torture rather than transgress the law of God.[3]

Still others, including Jeremiah, Paul, Silas, the pastor, and those known personally by the recipients of this letter – experienced mocking, scourging, chains, and imprisonment (Jeremiah 20:2; Acts 16:20-25; 2 Corinthians 11:23-25; Hebrews 10:32-35; 13:3)

> "Received trial" (Hebrews 11:36) implies that these people suffered such things as a trial or testing of their faithfulness to God and His promise.[4]

Jeremiah and Zechariah – were stoned to death (2 Chronicles 24:21; Jeremiah 44:24-27) "This was [Jeremiah's] fate, according to tradition, at the hands of the Jews in Egypt who could not abide his protest against their continuing idolatry."[5]

Isaiah – was sawn in two, according to Jewish tradition

Many prophets, Uriah, John the Baptist, James, and others – were put to death by the sword (1 Kings 19:10; Jeremiah 26:23; Daniel 11:33; Mark 6:25-28; Acts 12:2)

David, Elijah, Elisha, Ezekiel, Isaiah, John the Baptist, and others – wandered, wore sheepskins and goatskins, were destitute, afflicted, and tormented (Judges 6:2; 1 Samuel 23:14; 1 Kings 17:2-16; 19:1-19; 2 Kings 1:3-15; Ezekiel 1:1; 4:10-13; Matthew 3:1-3)

Who would you choose to interview and what would you ask them?

Who do you respect as a hero of faith who has endured great affliction? Try to name at least one person who is alive on earth and one person who is alive in Heaven!

What is the pastor's conclusion to his list of the heroes of faith? Write out Hebrews 11:40.

The promise that all those before us were looking toward has been fulfilled!

What does 2 Corinthians 1:20 say?

Hallelujah! The promise of the One who was to come, the promise of the Redeemer, the promise of blessings, the promise of the Deliverer, the promise of the New Covenant, the promise of forgiveness, the promise of being the holy people of God—has been fulfilled. God kept His promise through Christ. He has perfected us and all those who were looking to Him in faith.

> They and we together now enjoy unrestricted access to God through Christ, as fellow-citizens of the heavenly Jerusalem. The "better plan" which God had made embraces the better hope, the better promises, the better covenant, the better sacrifices, the better and abiding possession, and the better resurrection which is their heritage and ours.[6]

And so the pastor urges his readers and us not to settle for anything less than God's better plan. We too are to live by faith, depend on God's power, endure affliction, and look toward the future that God has promised us.

Now is the time for faith.

LESSON 38: ENDURE THE AGONY
HEBREWS 12: 1-3

In the 2016 Olympics, Usain Bolt was the fastest man alive, running the 100-meter dash at 9.58 seconds. If you were about to run a race at a track meet, wouldn't it be encouraging to have Bolt give you some tips and then cheer you on from the stands? This is the stuff of movies! That special person in the stands gives the athlete the wind beneath their wings when they think they just can't go on!

The pastor wants us to realize that those who have gone before us faced hardships and challenges as we do and they persevered to the end of their race. That is what we are to do.

Please pray that the Holy Spirit will energize you to endure suffering and keep your eyes on Jesus.

Please read Hebrews 12:1-3. Highlight all words and phrases that describe us and what we are to do.

^{NKJ} **Hebrews 12:1-3** Therefore we also, since we are surrounded by so great a cloud of witnesses, let us lay aside every weight, and the sin which so easily ensnares us, and let us run with endurance the race that is set before us, ²looking unto Jesus, the author and finisher of our faith, who for the joy that was set before Him endured the cross, despising the shame, and has sat down at the right hand of the throne of God. ³For consider Him who endured such hostility from sinners against Himself, lest you become weary and discouraged in your souls.

The first word is "therefore." This is a very important word! It moves us from one place to another. It leads us to a conclusion. It takes us to an action point. This is exactly what the pastor wants to do from Hebrews 11 to Hebrews 12.

He exhorts us to action, to keep moving to the goal ahead of us as the heroes before us did. He reminds us of the agonizing marathon that we also are in the midst of running. We are not the only ones who have a hard race.

The athletic imagery used in these verses is the same that was used often in Greek and Jewish rhetoric. Which words and phrases remind you of aspects of running a race?

Please look up the following words:
Cloud: Strong's #3505
Greek word:
Greek definition:

Witnesses: Strong's #3144
Greek word:
Greek definition:

Race: Strong's #73
Greek word:
Greek definition:

> **Agon:** *a place of assembly* (in Homer's Iliad); specifically, the place in which the Greeks assembled to celebrate solemn games (as the Pythian, the Olympian); hence, *a contest*, of athletes, runners, charioteers.[1]

> The comparison of life to engagement in an athletic contest was the common property of preachers of moral philosophy, whose sermons could be heard in the streets of every hellenistic town in the first century. The terms agon, "contest," and agonizesthai, "to strive," "to engage in a contest," evoked thoughts of tense exertion, maximum effort, and a constantly renewed concentration of energy on the attainment of the goal.[2]

We should think of the cloud of witnesses as a huge crowd in the seats of a stadium. However, verse 1 emphasizes what we—living believers—see surrounding us, rather than emphasizing that the heroes of faith are watching us. We see that God was faithful to them and that reminds us that God will be faithful to us.

What are we to do according to Hebrews 12:1?

This too is athletic imagery. "Contestants removed all of their clothing before running so that nothing could impede them during the race." [3] This was usually the long heavy robes worn by the Greeks, which would obviously have impeded running!

The pastor included the Greek word "panta" (every, all) as an important adjective. Anything and everything that would hinder a runner should be put aside. We can easily understand the parallel that the pastor is making for our Christian lives. Whatever might interfere with our commitment to Jesus Christ must be thrown off.

What are some things that might limit your service to the Lord? Or might handicap your testimony? Or make endurance difficult?

We are to notice those surrounding us who have gone before us, but we are to fix our eyes specifically in one direction and on one person.

According to Hebrews 12:2:

On whom do we keep our eyes?

What eternal title of accomplishment has been awarded to Him?

On what did He keep His focus?

What was the agony of His "race"?

What was His reward?

Reflect on the details included in the Hall of Faith of Hebrews 11. We saw names, circumstances, faithfulness, obedience, and the anticipation of rewards. There are many similarities between those heroes and Jesus.

What parallels are there between the life of Christ and the lives of the cloud of witnesses?

Briefly summarize Hebrews 2:9-18. Make sure you note the title given to Jesus in verse 10.

In Hebrews 6:20, Jesus is described as the "forerunner." This is an athletic term referring to "the swiftest runner who breaks away from the pack to cross the finish line first." [4]

When we look at Hebrews 2:9-19, 6:20, and 12:1-3 together, we can see that Jesus is the champion! The title given to Him in the first and third passages is the Greek word "archegon," which is defined as the one who goes first on the path and blazes the trail for others to follow. "In light of the athletic metaphor, it is proper to recognize in archegon the nuance of champion." [5]

What is the new trail that Jesus has blazed? What did He break through as He crossed the finish line? Base your answer on Hebrews 9:8-12 and Hebrews 10:19-20.

Have you been in any races? Running? Swimming? Biking? 3-legged races? Turtle races?! My son and daughter were on the track team in high school and both enjoyed a few victories. They are far better runners than I am. But even in the short distance that I try to run, I know how very important it is to look ahead toward my destination.

We are told by the pastor to keep our eyes on Jesus. Why are we to do this, according to Hebrews 12:3?

Perspective is so important. There is no one who has experienced more suffering than Jesus. And His suffering was absolutely undeserved. But just realizing that Jesus endured the worst suffering of all time is not what gives us strength. It is depending on His indwelling Spirit in us that enables us to endure.

Note the truths of the following verses:

2 Corinthians 12:9

Galatians 2:20

Hebrews 13:6

Jesus is the champion who initiates and perfects our faith. He lives in us by His Spirit and He urges us to keep running our race until we reach the finish line. That will be the beginning of a glorious eternity! Let us endure the agony and we will then enjoy the delight of eternity when we see Jesus face to face!

LESSON 39: For Our Good
Hebrews 12:4-11

In the last lesson, we saw that the pastor used the example of running in a race to encourage us toward endurance. I'd like to continue the use of athletic imagery as we study the next instructions in Hebrews 12:4-11. If we see ourselves as athletes, we will realize that we need a coach who will train us to be the best we can be. Some athletes have their own fathers as their trainers. Who else would have the very best intentions for an athlete than his own parent?

Please pray that the Holy Spirit will give you understanding of the ways that He corrects you.

Please read Hebrews 12:1-11.

What does Hebrews 12:4 tell us about the circumstances of the readers?

What they *are* experiencing –

What they *have not* experienced (yet) –

How it compares to the suffering of Christ (see verses 2 and 3) –

The readers were told to consider Jesus and what He experienced so that they could compare their suffering with His suffering on the cross. There is no comparison, is there? But fixing our eyes on Jesus makes us get our eyes off of ourselves. If we only look at our current situation, we will get discouraged and depressed which can even lead to physical fatigue and sickness.

What does the pastor say is a problem for his readers, according to Hebrews 12:5? Fill in the blanks below:

Hebrews 12:5 You have_____ the _____which is addressed to you as _____ .

The pastor had urged them early on in his letter—pay attention! Don't drift from the word spoken to you (Hebrews 2:1).

What was this very important word of encouragement from God that they had forgotten? The pastor quotes it for them, just as it was stated in Proverbs 3:11-12. It was so critical for the Hebrews then, and it is so critical for us now.

Please write the verses quoted in Hebrews 12:5-6. Because the pastor has explained that this is "addressed to you as sons," you should read it as the words of God Himself speaking to you. There are four statements made. Write them on the lines below.

1. _____

2. _____

3. _____

4. _____

Depending on your translation, you may have written the words chasten, discipline, rebuke, reprove, correct, punish, and scourge. So that we don't put our own preconceived ideas into the interpretation of this passage, we need to understand the words that were used.

Please look up the definition for the following words:
NAS Discipline / NKJ Chastening: Strong's #3809
Greek word:
Greek definition:

NAS Reprove / NKJ Rebuke: Strong's #1651
Greek word:
Greek definition:

NAS Scourge / NIV Punish : Strong's #3146
Greek word:
Greek definition:

Based on these words, which are given to us to encourage us, we must understand several points:

- <u>The Lord disciplines us.</u> *Based on the word "paideia," this means that He instructs, trains, corrects, and punishes us so that we will grow up into maturity.*

- *The Lord rebukes us. Based on the word "elegcho," this means that He convicts us of sin, shows us our faults, and admonishes us to correct us.*

- *The Lord punishes us. Based on the word "mastigo," this means that He uses suffering to train and correct us.*

> The biblical concept of discipline (*paideia*) combines the nuances of training, instruction, and firm guidance with those of reproof, corrections, and punishment. Adversity and hardships are to be recognized as means designed by God to call His people to faithful and obedient sonship. [1]

The pastor expounds on Proverbs 3 11-12 in Hebrews 12:7-11. Answer the questions below based on all of Hebrews 12:5-11.

What is communicated about the **relationship** between God the Father and His people?

What should our **attitude** be (or not be) regarding the discipline of the Lord?

What is the **purpose** of the discipline of the Lord?

> Satan wants us to believe that the difficulties of life are proof that God does not love us, but just the opposite is true. Sometimes God's chastening is seen in His rebukes from the Word or from circumstances. At other times He shows His love by punishing ("the Lord . . . scourgeth") us with some physical suffering.[2]

*Is this instruction about the discipline, reproof, and punishment of the Lord surprising to you? This study has opened my eyes to better understand the wisdom and ways of the Lord. I didn't understand that the Lord would **punish** me to correct and train me. But now I know better! As a Christian, as a child of God, I may experience painful suffering as punishment for my sin, and God's purpose in that suffering will be for my sanctification. He is always about growing me up into His likeness, into holiness.*

Let's make sure that we understand the difference between the punishment of God upon His children and the wrath of God against unbelievers.

What does John 3:36 say?

What does Romans 5:9 say?

And let's make sure that we understand that while Christians may suffer as punishment for their sins, sufferings are not always a punishment for sin.

What was the sin and punishment for it, according to Acts 5:3-10?

What was the sin and punishment for it, according to 1 Corinthians 11:27-32?

What was the sin and the suffering caused by it, according to James 4:1-4?

What was the suffering and what was the cause of it, according to Job 1:8-22?

What was the suffering and what was the cause of it, according to 1 Thessalonians 2:14-15?

What was the suffering and what was the purpose of it, according to 1 Peter 1:3-7?

Please read Hebrews 12:1-11 again. Summarize the instruction of this passage. You might want to think of it as what the coach wants for his favorite athlete. What does he need? What is his goal? Who is his example? What's it going to take to win the prize?

There is one more command to look at in this lesson. It's like a coach's order to his team. What does Hebrews 12:12-13 say?

The first verse is from Isaiah 35:3, and the next verse shows us the attitude adjustment necessary. What does Isaiah 35:4 say?

Perhaps the pastor didn't state verse 4 because he had already made it clear:

^{NAS} **Hebrews 10:30:** "For we know Him who said, "Vengeance is Mine, I will repay." And again, "The Lord will judge His people."

Hebrews 12:13 is based on Proverbs 4:25-27, of which the pastor may have been thinking. Note the instructions.

Here's how The Message paraphrases the pastor's pep talk:

> Don't sit around on your hands! No more dragging your feet! Clear the path for long-distance runners so no one will trip and fall, so no one will step in a hole and sprain an ankle. Help each other out. And run for it! ³

LESSON 40: CLEAR INSTRUCTIONS
Hebrews 12:14-17

Does it feel like the pastor is about to wrap up his sermon? Not if we look at the number of verses and topics ahead of us. However, we are actually at his final portion which will mainly include instructions, described by one commentator as: "orientation for life as Christians in a hostile world."¹

The instructions are clarified and illustrated by more examples from the Old Testament, which shouldn't surprise us! Above all, the pastor is urging his dear friends to continue, to press on, to keep moving forward in this pilgrimage toward the heavenly country, the city of God, to Mount Zion where all promises will ultimately be fulfilled.

Please pray that you will obey the voice of the Holy Spirit as you live one day at a time.

Please read Hebrews 12:14-13:25. This is the final portion of the pastor's sermon.

List the instructions given in the following verses:

Hebrews 12:14 a.

b.

Hebrews 12:15 a.

b.

Hebrews 12:16

Hebrews 12:25

Hebrews 12:28 a.

b.

Hebrews 13:1

Hebrews 13:2

Hebrews 13:3

Hebrews 13:4

Hebrews 13:5

Hebrews 13:7

Hebrews 13:9

Hebrews 13:13

Hebrews 13:14

Hebrews 13:15

Hebrews 13:16

Hebrews 13:17

Hebrews 13:18

Hebrews 13:22

Hebrews 13:24

It really is an orientation for life as Christians in a hostile world! I hope you could see the pastor's explanations and encouragements along the way as he detailed the way to live in the midst of persecution. His instructions are for every believer, but they are especially important for his readers who have been considering withdrawing from their Christian community.

Now that we've had an overview of the concluding comments, we'll look at them more closely over the next lessons, because there are some intriguing, shocking, and wonderful truths to grasp.

*The first instruction in Hebrews 12:14 is "strive for peace with everyone." This is not just a sweet sentiment. Because it is given as an important command, it probably indicates that there was disunity and friction in the Christian community. Remember, they were not to forsake the assembly, but fellowship together. And there was certainly a need to behave peaceably toward unbelievers who persecuted them. The **gospel** is offensive to some but **you** don't have to be!*

How can you strive for peace in your Christian community? What is your Christian community?

How can you pursue peace with unbelievers who are hostile toward you because of your faith?

What clear instruction is also given in connection with the command to pursue peace? See Hebrews 12:14, and note why it is important.

What did the pastor previously say would bring about holiness? See Hebrews 12:10.

Our holy God requires holiness in us. The word used in Hebrews 12:14 specifically refers to our sanctification and a practical holy lifestyle. It makes sense that the list of instructions that follow are those behaviors and attitudes that will be evidenced in our lives as we pursue holiness.

A book I read when I was in high school opened my eyes to everyday choices that I can make that will demonstrate my faith and love for the Lord. It was The Pursuit of Holiness *by Jerry Bridges, and I still have my original copy, with many notes and highlights.*

*Bridges entitles Chapter 3: "Holiness is not an Option" and quotes Hebrews 12:14. He points out that through Christ, we are **made** holy in our standing before God (Hebrews 10:10), and we who are made holy are **called** to be holy in our daily lives.[2]*

He then makes this comment:

> So the writer of Hebrews is telling us to take seriously the necessity of personal, practical holiness. When the Holy Spirit comes into our lives at our salvation, He comes to make us holy in practice. If there is not, then, at least a yearning in our hearts to live a holy life pleasing to God, we need to seriously question whether our faith in Christ is genuine.[3]

Give some examples of practical holiness. Is there evidence of it in your life? Do you desire it? Do you grieve over sinful behavior and desire to turn from it?

The next instructions are made very clear in the following translation.

NLT Hebrews 12:15 Look after each other so that none of you fails to receive the grace of God. Watch out that no poisonous root of bitterness grows up to trouble you, corrupting many.

What are some positive results of fellowship and accountability within our Christian community, based on this verse?

Some translations of Hebrews 12:15 might lead one to think that they could lose their salvation. The NKJV says, "lest anyone fall short of the grace of God." The NLT above is much better and indicates that we must make sure that we depend on all that the grace of God has already achieved for us. Wiersbe says, "God's grace does not fail, but we can fail to take advantage of His grace."[4]

What does the pastor say about grace? Record his statements in the verses below.

Hebrews 4:16

Hebrews 13:9

Hebrews 13:25

God's grace is amazing. Abundant. Saving. Sufficient. A gift. Greater than all our sin. Glorious and rich. Through it we receive salvation and through it we endure until we see our Savior.

To reinforce his instructions thus far, the pastor gives the readers an example of one who did not pursue peace and daily holiness but instead indulged himself in temporary gratification.

Read Hebrews 12:16-17. (If you want to read the whole story about Esau, see Genesis 25:27-34 and Genesis 27:34-41.)

Why is Esau described as immoral and unholy (ESV translation), according to verse 16?

> Esau typifies the godless person who relinquished the rights conferred upon him by the covenant for the sake of momentary relief. [5]

Esau didn't walk by faith. He didn't wait for the promises of God that were his as the firstborn. He didn't endure the suffering of the moment of hunger and fatigue. He lost the blessing that he could have had. The pastor's message was clear: Don't be like Esau!

> A believer can make a decision to disobey God for materialistic reasons and find it impossible to reverse the future consequences of that willful act. [6]

> Esau had to abide by the consequences of what he had brought upon himself. Yet he learned his lesson, for Esau called his firstborn Eliphaz, "strength of God," and his second son Reuel, "joy of God" (Genesis 36:10). [7]

Even though Esau forfeited the inheritance of his birthright, God gave him his own land in which to live, the territory known as Edom. Esau gave his sons names that honored God, and he eventually had a peaceful reunion with his brother Jacob.

What do the following verses tell us?

Mark 13:13

John 6:27-29

James 1:12

Do you need any attitude adjustments? Are you looking for a way out of momentary affliction, like Esau did, that would cause you to forfeit an eternal reward?

*Esau has been described by commentators as foolish. I would agree. Shortsighted. Reckless. I'm thankful for his example, however, of what **not** to do.*

No matter what the circumstances, I want to hold fast to Jesus, walk by faith, pursue holiness, and wait for the promises of God.

> Jim Elliot (1927-56) said: "God always gives His best to those who leave the choice with him." He was 28 years old when killed in Ecuador by Huaorani warriors, the very people with whom he wanted to share the gospel of Christ.[8]

WARNING – WARNING – WARNING

LESSON 41: UNSHAKEABLE
Hebrews 12:18-29

As we saw in our last lesson, the pastor gives us clear instructions with very practical, tangible applications for our everyday life. We are to live them out by faith. By grace. Pursuing holiness. And revering our holy God.

What will motivate us as we press on in the marathon of our spiritual journey? Will it be a look back at an ominous, smoking, quaking mountain of laws? Or will it be looking ahead to a mountain where we will find grace and celebration and the family of God, and God Himself?

The pastor will show us the contrast between Mount Sinai of the Old Covenant and Mount Zion of the New Covenant. One shakes, but the other is unshakeable. And we can be unshakeable too, even in hard times, when we continue forward toward all that Mount Zion offers us.

Please pray that the Holy Spirit will encourage you to press on in confidence based on the great grace of God.

Please read Hebrews 12:18-29.

As the pastor begins to conclude his sermon, he doesn't change the major emphasis of his teaching. What Jesus has made possible through His sacrifice and the New Covenant is much better than what was given before. The pastor used the imagery of two mountains to compare the difference between the Old and New Covenants once more. His word choice would have made quite an impact on those hearing the descriptions of them.

List the words and phrases that communicate the awesome and terrifying encounter at Mount Sinai, according to Hebrews 12:18-21.

This description is based on the pastor's summary of the account in Exodus 19:16-19; 20:18-21 and Deuteronomy 4:11-15. This is when the Lord gave the Mosaic Law, the Ten Commandments, and put the terms of the Old Covenant in place.

> The mountain was so charged with the holiness of the God who manifested Himself there that for man or beast to touch it meant certain death.[1]

What was the reaction of the Israelites when they saw and heard the manifestation of God at Mount Sinai, according to Hebrews 12:19-20?

The Israelites were at a real mountain which could be touched. They saw and heard real evidence of God in the smoke, fire, earthquake, and sounds. But they backed away from that awesome display of His power. They didn't draw near to Him.

> The Law was designed to put forth the requirements of righteousness and to create an awareness of personal guilt and fear. It did not provide the gracious means to bring condemned sinners into the presence of God.[2]

The pastor emphasizes that, "you have not come to the mountain that may be touched," and he declares, "but you have come to Mount Zion." This is the place of the New Covenant with much better offerings.

List the words and phrases that communicate the delightful experience at Mount Zion, according to Hebrews 12:22-24.

This description is based on a variety of Scriptures.

> Mount Zion was the site of the Jebusite stronghold which David captured and made his royal residence in the seventh year of his reign. He made it the religious center of his kingdom by installing there "the ark of God, which is called by the name of Yahweh of hosts, who sits enthroned on the cherubim" (2 Sam.6:2). Thus Zion became the earthly dwelling-place of God, "the city which Yahweh had chosen out of all the tribes of Israel, to put His name there" (1 Kings 14:21). When later Solomon built his temple on the hill to the north of Zion, and installed the sacred ark there, the name Zion was extended to include this further area, and became in practice synonymous with Jerusalem.[3]

How does Psalm 48 describe Mount Zion? Note that which corresponds to Hebrews 12:22-24.

How do the following verses describe Mount Zion, its inhabitants, and the presence of the Lord?

Isaiah 28:16

Isaiah 51:11

Isaiah 59:20

Daniel 7:10

Revelation 4:8-11

When we all . . . . get to heaven . . . . what a day of rejoicing that will be! Oh yes, it will. I am looking forward to it. By faith!

But until we all get there, the point of the description of Mount Zion, the heavenly Jerusalem, is that we already have what it holds for us. Through Christ, we have come to the dwelling place of our holy God. We have access to the holy of holies, His holy throne of grace. The privileges of our citizenship in heaven can be enjoyed right here, right now, on earth.

Praise God!

By the way, this is the city that Abraham and other heroes of faith were looking towards (Hebrews 11:10,14-17). The phrase, "the spirits of just men made perfect," in Hebrews 12:23 is understood by commentators to refer to Old Testament followers of God. They did not attain perfection until Christ came in the fullness of time and, "by one offering . . . brought those who are sanctified to perfection" (Hebrews 10:14; 11:40).[4]

It will be so exciting to be gathered together with all the saints of history.

But who is emphasized and why, according to Hebrews 12:24? It's important to note the detail in verse 24 because the exhortation in Hebrews 12:25 is based on it.

What 2 items speak in verse 24?

Who speaks in verse 25 and why is this speaking better?

The pastor's conclusion echoes his introduction. Note the similarities between the following verses:

INTRODUCTION	CONCLUSION
Hebrews 1:2	Hebrews 12:25
Hebrews 2:1-3	
Hebrews 1:10-12	Hebrews 12:26-27
	Hebrews 13:8

What is the prophecy that the pastor based his statements on? Note what is to come, according to Haggai 2:6-7.

> The prophets prediction of the coming new age associated with the shaking of the earth again signifies that the old order [Old Covenant] established with a shaking of the earth will be done away. Haggai's prophecy gave notice that the existing Levitical order was a temporary arrangement which ultimately would be terminated so that a permanent and unshakeable order may be instituted. The implication the writer made was that if his readers attempt to revert to Judaism to find refuge from affliction, they will be returning to that which would be done away.[5]

What is to be our response to receiving an unshakeable kingdom, according to Hebrews 12:28-29?

Through Jesus our Mediator, we have access to the permanent, unshakeable Kingdom of Light, Grace, and Love. The Kingdom of God and the Kingdom of Christ.

When your life is "all shook up," do you look to temporary fixes or the One who is unchangeable and unshakeable?

LESSON 42: PRECIOUS DOCTRINE AND PRACTICAL CONDUCT
HEBREWS 13:1-14

This written sermon to the Hebrews has explained many doctrinal truths which have been the basis for urging the readers to listen to, obey, have faith in, and hold fast to Jesus during all of life's circumstances.

> No doctrine is without its practical application, and the doctrine of the superiority of Christ is so forcefully presented in this letter that it will certainly affect the practical conduct of believers.[1]

We saw in an earlier lesson that the instructions in Hebrews 12 and 13 give us an orientation for life as Christians in a hostile world. And at the end of our last lesson we saw that because we have grace as citizens of an unshakeable kingdom, we may serve God acceptably with reverence and godly fear.

With his concluding exhortations, the pastor will wrap it all up. He has truly presented precious doctrine and those truths should result in practical conduct.

Please pray that you will hear the truths taught by the Holy Spirit and heed His instructions for your daily activities.

Please read Hebrews 13:1-25.

There are many ways to show brotherly love. What is specifically mentioned and what reasons are given, according to Hebrews 13:1-3?

Brotherly love is the translation of the Greek word "philadelphia." This word refers specifically to the love of one Christian for his brother or sister in the faith. It is never used biblically of natural love between children of the same parents or of a believer's love for the unsaved.[2]

Review the exhortations of Hebrews 3:13 and Hebrews 10:24-25. Why is the concluding appeal for brotherly love so important?

In Hebrews 13:4, why is there a clear, practical affirmation of marriage as honorable? And even more specifically that the marriage bed is undefiled? The pastor brings up this point because he knew that somebody needed to hear this clear teaching.

> The author thus charged that marriage should be "honorable" (timios), a prized possession worthy of respect in all situations of life. Sexual acts within the marital union are not sinful. Married believers must always meet the sexual needs of their partners (1 Corinthians 7:3-5). God will judge the violators of proper sexual behavior.[3]

Please read Hebrews 13:5-6. The statements in these verses belong together. One verse may be challenging, while the other is certainly comforting. Think about and note how contentment is related to knowing the presence and help of Jesus.

Please notice that while the pastor has urged us through his sermon that we not forsake each other and not turn away from the Lord, he also declares to us that the Lord Himself will not let go of us. We hold fast to Jesus, but He holds on to us with a grip that will never ever slip.

We've seen many examples to follow throughout the sermon. Who are we to observe carefully and imitate, according to Hebrews 13:7? What should you look for in a leader based on this verse? Describe an example of a leader that you have had the privilege to exemplify.

God gives us good shepherds to watch over us and guide us. But there is still One who is better than any godly leader on earth. Let's pause and rejoice in the eternality of Jesus Christ.

Write Hebrews 13:8.

What did Jesus do for us "yesterday"? See Hebrews 5:7.

What does Jesus do for us "today"? See Hebrews 8:1, 9:24.

What does Jesus do for us "forever"? See Hebrews 7:24-25.

Our God and Savior is exalted for Who He is and what He does—forever! I am thrilled that you and I will experience the exceeding riches of His grace and kindness in all the ages to come.

How will creation respond to our God and Savior, according to Revelation 5:11?

That's the way things should be. But all things have not yet submitted to the authority of our God. So we must be careful.

What practical conduct is necessary, according to Hebrews 13:9?

We can learn from this verse that false teaching (1) promotes false doctrine; (2) emphasizes externals, i.e. foods; and (3) produces no effective spiritual results.[4] There is no profit for a believer in following false teachers. But it sure does seem like false teachers make a profit in their false teaching.

> The pastor began by urging his hearers not to "drift away" through "neglect" of God's great salvation in Christ (Heb. 2:1-4). He concludes by warning them not to allow themselves "to be carried away with diverse and strange teachings." Instead, through Christ they are to move upward into God's presence and forward with perseverance.[5]

What truths are emphasized in Hebrews 13:10-12? The pastor reminds his readers once again of the activity of the Great High Priest.

> "We have an altar" (Heb. 13:10) does not suggest a material altar on earth, for that would contradict the whole message of the epistle. A new covenant Christian's altar is Jesus Christ, for it is through Him that we offer our "spiritual sacrifices" to God (Heb. 13:15). We may set aside places in our church buildings and call them altars, but they are really not altars in the biblical sense. Why? Because Christ's sacrifice has already been made, once and for all, and the gifts that we bring to God are acceptable, not because of any earthly altar, but because of a heavenly altar, Jesus Christ.[6]

What are we exhorted to do and why, according to Hebrews 13:13-14?

> The readers of this epistle were looking for a way to continue as Christians while escaping the persecution that would come from unbelieving Jews. "It cannot be done," the writer states in so many words. "Jerusalem is doomed. Get out of the Jewish religious system and identify with the Savior who died for you." There can be no room for compromise.[7]

You probably don't need to get out of Jerusalem, but is there something that you have been clinging to that you should let go of so that you will fully identify with Jesus Christ? Are you straddling the fence on any issues or behaviors to avoid ridicule for your faith?

"Here we have no continuing city, but we seek the one to come." What a precious truth. What a statement of reality and of faith. What a hope and what a journey we still have ahead of us!

There are just a few more comments from the pastor and they will be just what we need to hear to stay on course toward our destination. Don't drift. There's a better harbor on the horizon.

LESSON 43: UNTIL THEN
HEBREWS 13:15-25

Are we there yet? Not yet. None of us know the day that we will finish our time on earth and move to our eternal heavenly home. But we aren't supposed to stand around twiddling our thumbs here while we wait. There's plenty to do!

Please pray that you will yield to the Holy Spirit and obey all of the words of God.

Please read Hebrews 13:15-25.

What are we to do continually and how are we to do it, according to Hebrews 13:15-16? How does the pastor define sacrifice in these verses?

Do you find one type of sacrifice easier than another? What do sacrifices of praise look like in your life? Do you sacrifice property and service for others in the name of Jesus?

> Christianity is sacrificial through and through; it is founded on the one self-offering of Christ, and the offering of His people's praise and property, of their service and their lives, is caught up into the perfection of His acceptable sacrifice, and is accepted in Him.[1]

What else are we to do as we continue on our journey toward the city of God, according to Hebrews 13:17-19?

What's good for the goose is good for the gander. Or maybe we should say: what's good for the sheep is good for the shepherd! Do you want your pastors and leaders to teach God's Word, guide wisely, warn of danger, and encourage holiness? Our submission to them will give them joy and give us growth.

What are some ways you can show honor and submission to your leaders?

Because the pastor writing his friends asked for prayer, let's take this occasion and pray for our own pastors and leaders.

We've come to the closing prayer and final words of the pastor to the Hebrews. It's loving and meaningful and so very encouraging. It's a final reminder of the doctrine of the superiority of Jesus Christ and the response we should have to Who He is.

Please read Hebrews 13:20-25.

Remember that the pastor chooses every word carefully and writes not only with eloquence, but also with an emphasis on what is most important.

List the 8 phrases of the prayer in Hebrews 13:20-21 that summarize the teachings of the book of Hebrews.

Now may _____

Who _____

That great _____

Through the _____

Equip you _____

Working in _____

Through _____

To Whom be _____

Each of the phrases above communicates the precious truths and exhortations that the pastor has shared throughout his sermon.

Look at the concepts below and write the appropriate one next to the phrase it corresponds to above. Record what you learn from the cross-references.

Fellowship

    Colossians 1:19-20

Resurrection power

    Ephesians 1:19-20

Care and provision

    John 10:11-14

    1 Peter 2:25

Forgiveness and access to God

    Matthew 26:28

Sanctification and obedience

    2 Corinthians 9:8

    Ephesians 2:10

    1 John 2:17

Faith and holiness

    Hebrews 11:6

    1 Thessalonians 3:13

The source of our strength and salvation

    John 16:23-24

    Ephesians 2:18

Eternal exaltation

    Philippians 2:11

Is this prayer in Hebrews 13:20-21 one that you pray often? There are several other prayers in the New Testament that I am much more familiar with and have prayed repeatedly. I am delighted to be more intimately acquainted with the pastor's closing prayer and all that it communicates. I will express it as the desire of my heart more often now.

Here are a few more comments about this deeply meaningful and passionate prayer.

Highlight that which is especially meaningful to you.

The God of peace – has opened the way to fellowship with Himself through the high-priestly work of Christ. This restoration of fellowship is the basis for a life of peace and wholeness within the community of God's people.

Who brought up our Lord Jesus from the dead – the pastor has made it clear that Christ has delivered His people from the fear of death (2:14-15) and that the faithful who seek the eternal City now live in anticipation of the resurrection.

That great Shepherd of the sheep – leads God's people into the heavenly homeland. He is not merely One who has opened the way but One who is ever present, shepherding His people toward their divinely promised goal by providing timely grace as they approach God through the One who is also their High Priest.

The blood of the eternal covenant – this phrase encapsulates the teaching of Hebrews on Christ's high priesthood. The blood refers to His faithful incarnate obedience, culminating in the offering of Himself for sin with all of the suffering and shame His self-offering entailed. This covenant is eternal because it is effective and will never need replacing.

Equip you with every good thing to do His will – "every good thing" is a comprehensive description of all the good things (9:11, 10:1) brought by Christ's high-priestly ministry. Thus, it includes cleansing from sin (9:14), a heart ready to obey (10:15-18), continual access into God's presence for succor in time of need (4:14-16), and the promise of entrance into an unshakeable Kingdom (12:28).

Working in us that which is pleasing in His sight – this phrase reminds us that we do not and cannot live this type of life on our own. God does not equip His people in such a way that they no longer need Him. He is continually doing or accomplishing this life in His people as they continually rely on Him and draw near through their High Priest.

Through Jesus Christ, to Whom be glory forever and ever – from beginning to end all is God's work in Christ. Glory is due forever to this God and to His Son, Who has become the source of eternal salvation (5:9).[2]

The pastor has poured out his heart in his sermon and in his prayer. He has been teaching us that through our great High Priest, we have open access to our holy God, upon Whom we can depend in all circumstances. So let us take action and enjoy the presence of God.

Personalize the prayer in Hebrews 13:20-21 and make your praises and requests known to our Father in Heaven through Jesus our Savior.

Please read Hebrews 13:22-25.

What is most intriguing to you about the pastor's final personal remarks?

I like this comment from Cockerill: "The information given demonstrates the intimate relationship between sender and recipients but is tantalizingly insufficient to establish with certainty their identity or location." ³

The last remarks seem like a "p.s."—just a few more personal details that the pastor wanted to communicate. Even in them, he encourages the believers to hear and obey the word of God.

The last comments don't answer the question of who wrote the sermon, except that they do rule out Timothy as the author! The greeting of those "from Italy" doesn't even confirm that the pastor was in Italy at the time of writing. There were many believers who fled from Italy under persecution, such as Aquila and Priscilla (Acts 18:2), and they may have been with the pastor at the time of his writing.

We still have tantalizing questions about the pastor and his flock. But the overwhelming message of his sermon can be summed up with one word.

What word is used in Hebrews 13:25 that summarizes the New Covenant and the work of our High Priest, Jesus Christ? Explain why this word is appropriate.

For a review of the message of grace throughout the sermon, note the phrases that refer to grace in the following verses:

Hebrews 2:9

Hebrews 4:16

Hebrews 10:29

Hebrews 12:15

Hebrews 13:9

Thank God for His amazing grace through Jesus Christ, the Source of our Eternal Salvation.

LESSON 44: JESUS IS BETTER
REFLECTIONS ON HEBREWS

Our study began with questions about the book of Hebrews. "Who wrote it?" is often the first thought when this book is mentioned. As I have encountered this question myself, I have reflected on what I know about the author of this letter.

He knows Jesus! And he depends on Jesus Christ as his compassionate High Priest who has accomplished everything necessary for him to be accepted by God. He knows that Jesus is superior to everyone and everything that might appear to be of help to us.

While there are a variety of topics addressed in this sermon, with many historical references and some unanswered questions, there is a consistent focus on the One who is better. The One who is the best.

Let's review the book of Hebrews by noting the truths given about Jesus Christ in the following verses. This page and the next list every verse that mentions the name of Jesus.

Hebrews 2:9

Hebrews 3:1

Hebrews 4:14

Hebrews 6:20

Hebrews 7:22

Hebrews 10:10

Hebrews 10:19

Hebrews 12:2

Hebrews 12:24

Hebrews 13:8

Hebrews 13:12

Hebrews 13:20-21

Isn't He wonderful? Isn't He amazing? Isn't He better than anyone or anything?

Summarize what you have learned from the book of Hebrews, perhaps using the truths about Jesus above as reminders. I encourage you to read the entire sermon to the Hebrews!

What has been the most applicable teaching for you from the sermon to the Hebrews?

Because the pastor described his letter as a "brief word of exhortation," which exhortation has been the most challenging? Encouraging? Difficult?

*I never want my last words in my workbooks to be **my** words, but instead the words of the Lord. God has spoken to us through His Son and through His Spirit! Please end this study with words between you and your Lord.*

Let's close as the pastor did, with his precious and passionate prayer:

^CSB **Hebrews 13:20-21** Now may the God of peace, who brought up from the dead our Lord Jesus—the great Shepherd of the sheep—with the blood of the everlasting covenant, ²¹equip you with all that is good to do His will, working in us what is pleasing in His sight, through Jesus Christ, to whom be glory forever and ever.

Amen.

ENDNOTES

Lesson 1
1. Lane, William L. *Hebrews 1-8, Volumes 1-8: Word Biblical Commentary*. Word Books, 1991, xlvii.

Lesson 2
1. Cockerill, Gareth Lee The *Epistle to the Hebrews, Volume 29 of The New International Commentary on the New Testament*. Wm. B. Eerdmans Publishing, 2012, 88.
2. Bruce, F.F. *The Epistle to the Hebrews*. William B. Eerdmans Publishing Company, 1990, 48.
3. Lane, 13.
4. Bruce, 49.
5. Bruce, 50.
6. Guthrie, George H. *Hebrews: The NIV Application Commentary*. Zondervan, 1998, 53.

Lesson 3
1. Guthrie, 67.
2. Bruce, 56.
3. Guthrie, 70.
4. Guthrie, 72.
5. Guthrie, 72.

Lesson 4
1. Murray, Andrew *The Holiest of All*. Whitaker House, 2004, 63.
2. Murray, 64.
3. Cockerill, 100.
4. *Fairest Lord Jesus* Anonymous, German: 17th century.

Lesson 5
1. Lane, 35.
2. Lane, 37.
3. Wiersbe, Warren *Be Confident: Live by Faith, Not by Sight, New Testament Commentary on Hebrews*. David C. Cook, 1982, 31.

Lesson 6
1. Guthrie, 19.
2. Wiersbe, 19.
3. Spicq, Ceslas *"L'Epitre aux Hébreux*. Paris: J. Gabalda, 1977.
4. Guthrie, 28.
5. Wiersbe, 20-21.

Lesson 7
1. Lane, 48.
2. Cockerill, 124.

Lesson 8
1. Friberg, Barbara and Timothy Friberg, Neva F. Miller *Analytical Lexicon of the Greek New Testament*. Baker's Greek New Testament Library, Baker Books, 2000, BibleWorks v.7.
2. Study note on Hebrews 2:14 in NET Bible. Biblical Studies Press, 2003.
3. Adapted from www.everydaychristian.com/blogs/hristmas_classics_the_man_and_the_birds_by_paul_harvey
4. Wiersbe, 39.

Lesson 9
1. www.jewishencyclopedia.com/articles/7689-high-priest
2. Henry, Matthew *Matthew Henry Commentary*. BibleWorks v.7, Hebrews - Chapter 3.
3. Friberg, BibleWorks v.7.

Lesson 10
1. Cockerill, 184.
2. Cockerill, 187.
3. Friberg, BibleWorks v.7.
4. Kent, Homer A. *The Epistle to the Hebrews: A Commentary*. BMH Books, 1972, 73.

Lesson 11
1. Lane, 101-102.
2. Lane, 99.
3. Lane, 102.

Lesson 12
1. Macarthur, J. and Mayhue, R. editors. *Biblical Doctrine: A Systematic Summary of Biblical Truth*. Crossway, 2017, 77.

2. Macarthur, 91.
3. Hodge, Charles *Systematic Theology* Wm. B. Eerdmans Publishing, 1940.
4. Grudem, Wayne A. *Systematic Theology: An Introduction to Biblical Doctrine* Zondervan Academic, 2009, 127.
5. Chicago Statement on Biblical Inerrancy (1978).
6. Macarthur, 114.
7. *Holy Bible, Book Divine*, John Burton, Sr , Youth's Mon-i-tor in Verse, 1803.

Lesson 13
1. Cockerill, 222.
2. Cockerill, 223.
3. Lane, 94.

Lesson 14
1. Howard, Kevin and Marvin Rosenthal *The Feasts of the Lord*, Zion's Hope, 1996, 119.
2. Wiersbe, 59.

Lesson 15
1. Gromacki, Robert *Stand Bold in Grace: An Exposition of Hebrews.* Kress Christian Publishers, 2001, 98.
2. Wiersbe, 74.
3. Lane, 132.

Lesson 16
1. Wiersbe, 78-79.
2. Wiersbe, 78-79.
3. Wiersbe, 78-79.
4. Thayer, Joseph Henry, translator *Greek-English Lexicon of the New Testament*. Harper, 1889; BibleWorks, v.7.
5. Gromacki, 110.

Lesson 17
1. Gromacki, 111.
2. Wiersbe, 80.

Lesson 18
1. *Father Abraham* [Recorded by Cedarmont Kids], (1997), On Action Bible Songs. Provident Music Group.
2. Bruce, 154.
3. Bruce, 154.
4. Bruce, 155.

Lesson 19
1. Only Ancestry combines DNA results and the largest collections of records. Retrieved from www.ancestry.com
2. Macarthur, 938.
3. Macarthur, 938.
4. Kent, 126.

Lesson 20
1. Thayer, BibleWorks, v.7.

Lesson 21
1. Cockerill, 346.
2. Cockerill, 346.
3. Cockerill, 347.
4. Pentecost, J. Dwight, and Kenneth M. Durham *Faith That Endures: A Practical Commentary on the Book of Hebrews*. Kregel Publications, 1992, 134.
5. Guthrie, 282.
6. Bruce, 197.

Lesson 22
1. Study note on Leviticus 18:1–30, in *Complete Jewish Bible: Illuminating the Jewishness of God's Word*. Barry Rubin, editor, translated by David H. Stern. Hendrickson Publishers Marketing, LLC, 2017, 1742.
2. Wiersbe, 118.
3. Kent, 164.
4. Study note on Leviticus 18:1–30, in *Complete Jewish Bible*, 1740.
5. Pentecost, 141.
6. Pentecost, 141.
7. Pentecost, 141.
8. Wiersbe, 119.

9. Lane, 226.
10. Guthrie, 284.
11. Pentecost, 143.

Lesson 23
1. Saphir, Adoph *The Epistle to the Hebrews: An Exposition, Volume 2.* Gospel Publishing House, 1902, 570.
2. Saphir, 574.

Lesson 24
1. Gromacki, 155.

Lesson 25
1. Cockerill, 423.
2. Cockerill, 416.
3. Cockerill, 426.

Lesson 26
1. Cockerill, 347.
2. Beale, G. K. and D. A. Carson, editors. *Commentary on the New Testament Use of the Old Testament.* Baker Books, 2007, 975.
3. Cockerill, 434.
4. Bruce, 240.

Lesson 27
1. Cockerill, 452.

Lesson 29
1. The Urban Dictionary says that hold fast means: to bear down. Retrieved from www.urbandictionary.com/define.php?term=hold%20fast
2. Friberg, BibleWorks, v.7.
3. Cockerill, 477.
4. Story of *Eternal Father, Strong to Save* as given by Eric Metaxas. Retrieved from www.breakpoint.org/2015/11/story-behind-navy-hymn.
5. *Eternal Father, Strong to Save.* Written by William Whiting, 1860, set to music by Rev. John Dykes.

Lesson 30
1. Guthrie, 345.
2. Saphir, 675.

Lesson 31
1. Thayer, BibleWorks, v.7.
2. Jamieson, Robert and Andrew Robert Fausset, David Brown *Jamieson, Fausset and Brown's Commentary on the Whole Bible.* Zondervan, 1961, www.e-sword.net.
3. Strong, James *Strong's Exhaustive Concordance of the Bible.* Henrickson Publishers, 2009, www.e-sword.net.
4. Gromacki, 174.
5. Gromacki, 175.
6. *My hope is built on nothing less than Jesus' blood and righteousness.* Edward Mote (1797-1874)

Lesson 32:
1. Bruce, 272.
2. Bruce, 277.
3. Bruce, 277.
4. Gromacki, 171.
5. Wiersbe, 143.
6. Gromacki, 183..
7. Cockerill, 520.

Lesson 33
1. Bruce, 282.
2. Bruce, 283.
3. Bruce, 287.
4. *Find us Faithful.* Written by Larry Mayfield and John Mohr. [Recorded by Steve Green] (1994), On People Need the Lord. Sparrow Records.

Lesson 34
1. Cockerill, 538.
2. Cockerill, 536.
3. Cockerill, 536.
4. Wiersbe, 148.
5. Cockerill, 563.

Lesson 35
1. Cockerill, 571.
2. Cockerill, 572.
3. Bruce, 317.

Lesson 36
1. Guthrie, 383.
2. Bruce, 321.
3. Barnes, Albert *Barnes' Notes on the New Testament.* Kregel Publications, 1962, www.e-sword.net

Lesson 37
1. Bruce, 323.
2. Bruce, 323.
3. Bruce, 325.
4. Cockerill, 593.
5. Bruce, 327.
6. Bruce, 330.

Lesson 38
1. *Thayer,* BibleWorks, v.7.
2. Lane, 408.
3. Lane, 409.
4. Lane, 410.
5. Lane, 411.

Lesson 39
1. Lane, 420.
2. Wiersbe, 162.
3. Peterson, Eugene *THE MESSAGE: The Bible in Contemporary Language.* NavPress, 1995.

Lesson 40
1. Lane, 431.
2. Bridges, Jerry *The Pursuit of Holiness.* NavPress, 1978, 38.
3. Bridges, 38.
4. Wiersbe, 164.
5. Lane, 455.
6. Gromacki, 208.
7. Lockyer, Herbert *All the Men of the Bible.* Zondervan Publishing House, 1958, 114.
8. God always gives His best to those who leave the choice with him. Retrieved from www.leadershipresources.org/blog/christian-missionary-jim-elliot-quotes

Lesson 41
1. Bruce, 354.
2. Gromacki, 209.
3. Bruce, 355.
4. Bruce, 360.
5. Pentecost, 213.

Lesson 42
1. Pentecost, 214.
2. Gromacki, 214.
3. Gromacki, 216.
4. Gromacki, 219.
5. Cockerill, 692.
6. Wiersbe, 178.
7. Wiersbe, 179.

Lesson 43
1. Bruce, 384.
2. Cockerill, 715-719.
3. Cockerill, 711.

PRAYER REQUESTS AND PRAISES

PRAYER REQUESTS AND PRAISES

PRAYER REQUESTS AND PRAISES

PRAYER REQUESTS AND PRAISES

PRAYER REQUESTS AND PRAISES

PRAYER REQUESTS AND PRAISES

PRAYER REQUESTS AND PRAISES

PRAYER REQUESTS AND PRAISES

PRAYER REQUESTS AND PRAISES

PRAYER REQUESTS AND PRAISES

PRAYER REQUESTS AND PRAISES

PRAYER REQUESTS AND PRAISES

Other Studies by Elizabeth Bagwell Ficken

Immeasurably More!: An in-depth study of Ephesians

Do you want your walk with Christ to be more intimate, more faithful, and more obedient? God is able to do immeasurably more than you can imagine through His power in your life! This exciting study will help you understand the never-ending blessings of salvation and the extraordinary potential you have to live a victorious and faithful Christian life.

That You May Know the Lord: An in-depth study of Ezekiel

Don't miss this great book! As you study this intriguing prophecy, you will be humbled by the holiness, sovereignty, and glory of God; you will be challenged to examine your own lives as you see the sin of the Israelites; you will be inspired as you see the power of the Holy Spirit; and you will be excited as you anticipate wonderful promises to be fulfilled by the Lord.

Follow Me: An in-depth study of the Gospel of Matthew

This study will challenge you to a more passionate commitment to Jesus. Learn from Matthew's eye-witness perspective, his proofs from Old Testament scriptures, and his presentation of Jesus' five sermons, just who Jesus is, what He did, and what He said. Matthew's life was drastically changed from his encounter with Jesus — yours will be too.

Come Let Us Worship: An in-depth study of Psalms

The Psalms contain many of our most well-known Scriptures, offering comfort and expressing the emotions of our souls. They challenge us to godly living, always trusting the Lord. What a beautiful arrangement of poems, prayers, and praises God has given us! From Psalm 1 to Psalm 150, you'll study selected psalms in the order of their placement in the Scriptures.

And the Lord Blessed Job: An in-depth study of Job

One of the Lord's blessings to Job was that he was chosen to show Satan that God is worthy of worship no matter what happens in our lives. While the book of Job deals with suffering, it isn't about answering the question "why do people suffer?" It's about humbly submitting to God as the Holy One who is infinite in wisdom, power, justice, and goodness.

Letters to the Thessalonians: An in-depth study of 1st and 2nd Thessalonians

These letters are about faith, hope, and love; holiness, prayer, and perseverance; the will of God and the glorious return of Christ. And so much more! Almost every major doctrine of our faith is covered in these personal writings from the apostle Paul. Join me as we read someone else's mail. I'm sure you'll find a few things that you will think were written just to you!

Find her! elizabethficken.com or

Available at **amazon.com** and other bookstores

www.ingramcontent.com/pod-product-compliance
Lightning Source LLC
Chambersburg PA
CBHW080435110426
42743CB00016B/3171